MW01247922

ABOVE THE ILLUSION

THE BLUEPRINT FOR MENTAL CLARITY, SELF-RESPECT, AND IRREPLACEABLE VALUE.

ANTHONY G. MINAYA

A. MINAYA ENTERPRISES, LLC

To Mami & Papi: Thank you for everything. I love you!

Broza!! From the four walls and the cracked floors to the book stores. Pur?ose baby!!

Come ons kid. You see this?!?! I told you.

CONTENTS

INTRODUCTION

ALL OF YOUR PSYCHOLOGICAL PAIN COMES FROM THE MEMORIES YOU RETAIN AND THE STORIES YOU CREATE

The mind you're using to read these words has been shaped since birth by everything you've encountered—your environment, your upbringing, the culture you've lived in, your education, the media you've consumed, and the beliefs you've absorbed along the way. You've been conditioned to accept certain truths without question, to fit into roles, to follow paths that were paved by others, not by your own conscious choices. This conditioning isn't something you're entirely aware of. It operates in the background, silently shaping your thoughts, your reactions, and the way you navigate life.

Think about it: how much of what you believe is something you truly examined for yourself? How often have you questioned the things you accept as truth? How much of your daily behavior is automatic? How many times do you react to situations without fully thinking them through, relying instead on habits formed over years of conditioning? Whether it's the way you handle stress, the way you approach relationships, or the way you feel about yourself, so much of it is pre-programmed. Your mind is doing what it's been trained to do, even if it's no longer serving you. Your beliefs about success, love, happiness, and purpose were absorbed from those around you, from society, and from a world that was shaping your mind before you even knew it. You've been playing out roles and patterns that were handed to you by your family, your friends, your culture, your social surroundings—they've all been part of the conditioning process.

As a child, you didn't have the awareness to question what you were taught. You simply just accepted it. And as you grew, those beliefs—those conditioned patterns— became part of who you thought you were. This foundation has shaped how you approach every aspect of your life. Think about how you define success. Is it based on what you actually want, or is it based on society's idea of achievement? How do you approach relationships? Do you believe in certain dynamics because you've truly examined them, or because you've been taught to see love and partnership in a specific way? How do you deal with failure? Is it something to fear because you've been conditioned to avoid it at all costs, or is it something to embrace as part of growth? A mind that refuses to question itself is a lost mind. It's a mind that is always living in fear because it is always confused about its current state. This is why most people hold on to their old patterns even when they're destructive—because the conditioning has made them feel safe, even if that safety is an illusion.

I was born and raised in The Bronx, New York, an environment that's both tough and full of culture. The Bronx is the birthplace of hip-hop, and you can feel the influence of the culture everywhere—from the graffiti to people blasting music at 3 A.M. in the morning, the food, the art, the music—it's all raw and real. But alongside the culture, there's also a constant presence of fear. This fear isn't just about physical danger, it's about the fear of never breaking free from the limitations that surround you. The fear that you'll never rise above the poverty, the broken system, the generational cycles of mediocrity.

The fear that no matter how hard you try, the world has already decided your fate. People grow up with this weight on their shoulders, feeling like they're constantly fighting to survive, to be seen, to be heard, but always with that nagging fear in the back of their minds that they're not going to make it. It's the fear of falling behind while others seem to get ahead, the fear that opportunities are out there but way out of reach. It's the fear that you'll end up like the people around you who've settled and given up on their dreams. This fear seeps into the soul and breeds a mindset of survival—just getting by becomes the goal.

This limits your vision, makes you think small, and keeps you from believing that there's something more. You become desensitized to the environment. The roaches, mice, dirty sidewalks, smelly train stations, and elevators filled with piss are all just normal everyday life. The mediocrity around you sinks into the foundation of your mind and you start to believe this is all life has to offer. When you're surrounded by people who have settled, who've accepted their fate, who live in survival mode every single day, it's easy to adopt the same mindset. It becomes normal to lower your standards.

This is why most people don't make it out of their situation because they don't believe there's anything to make it out of. They get swallowed up by the environment. They can't even recognize that there *is* a way out. It's like living in a cage with the door open but being too conditioned to see the exit. This is a victim mentality in its purest form. It's the belief that life is happening to you, that you're powerless, that the system is rigged and there's nothing you can do about it. When you believe you're the victim, you stop fighting. You stop dreaming. You settle into the routines of the people around you—the drugs, the violence, the quick highs, and the quick money.

Some people are doing just enough to put food on the table, pay the rent, and numb themselves with alcohol and entertainment in hopes it all gets better. This may make you feel good for the moment but in actuality you're getting further and further away from seeing yourself. The illusion of comfort and security is a trap. You get stuck in a cycle of survival and that survival mindset is a prison. You're never truly thriving. You're never really growing. You're just existing. And for many, that's enough. They don't see anything wrong with it because this may have been all they've ever known. It's what their parents knew, what their grandparents knew. It's generational. You grow up thinking, *"This is life,"* because no one told you otherwise, and even if someone attempted to tell you, many people in this situation would get offended because the truth was spoken. That's how conditioned the victim mindset is: There's a problem for every solution.

Psychological struggle isn't exclusive to any specific group of people. There are people that come from wealthy backgrounds, who on the surface, seem like they have it all —money, comfort, the best education—yet they are in conflict psychologically because everything was given to them growing up. They never developed the mental toughness to deal with life's challenges because they were sheltered from them. They grew up protected in comfort, but comfort breeds complacency and complacency dulls the mind. Their minds have become numb and disconnected. Conditioned by ease. Conditioned by a lack of struggle. They may not face survival in the same way, but their battles are internal—dealing with depression, meaninglessness, and anxiety despite the luxuries. When everything is handed to you, the drive to build something for yourself can disappear. This is why you see rich kids turning to drugs or losing themselves in reckless behavior—because they've never had to fight for anything real. Their struggle is a lack of struggle, and it can be just as damaging.

No matter where you come from, the foundation of the problems are all the same. The fact is, you have a choice. You can accept the conditions around you, or you can challenge them. My environment inspired me to dig deeper. I've always asked myself: Does it have to be this way? Do I just accept this life? Am I really this wack? I became obsessed with wanting to understand the process of the mind. I started noticing how everything was connected, how every small detail told a story, the way people spoke, the way they dressed, walked, stood, what they were willing to accept—it all revealed something deeper about their inner world. It was like these details were windows into their minds, showing me who they were without them even knowing it. The slouch in their posture, the hesitation in their speech, the way their eyes drifted away during a conversation—all of it pointed to something bigger. And the more I observed, the more I realized: The inner and outer world are one. There is no division.

A person's habits, their body language, their energy— all of it was a reflection of how they see themselves and the world. I started breaking down my own mindset, my own habits, and saw the truth for what it was: Most of my problems were self-made. The limitations, the frustrations, the excuses—they were by-products of my own perspective. I realized I had been accepting limits that didn't even exist. And from that point forward, I made a decision to completely transform my life.

But not in a surface level way like most people do. I

didn't want to just read a self help book, change careers, meet new friends, change how I dress, and call it growth. I wanted real transformation. I wanted to see what would happen if I dedicate my life to becoming the absolute best version of myself. So I started doing the work. I became my own experiment.

I started upgrading every part of myself—physically, mentally, emotionally, financially. I started looking at myself from the inside out, paying attention to the thoughts I entertained, the habits I had formed, and the ways I reacted to the world. I took ownership of everything, no longer blaming my circumstances or the people around me, but recognizing that I was responsible for my growth. I questioned everything about who I was, about what I believed, about what I thought was possible for me.

Every detail mattered. The way I started my day, the way I interacted with others, what I consumed, the way I reacted to challenges—all of it was a reflection of who I was and who I was becoming. I asked myself the hard questions: What am I afraid of? Why am I settling for less than I'm capable of? What's really holding me back? Can people like me actually win? I wanted to see the truth about myself. This is the foundation of how I live my life today. I'm a forever project, always evolving, always leveling up, always studying.

At the time of writing this book, I've spent over 15 years working with people, helping them shift their perspective and become the best version of themselves. I've personally worked with hundreds of individuals one-on-one, and I've helped thousands of people online to transform their lives. I've dedicated my life to studying, researching, and understanding the mind and human behavior. This is my life's work. It's a reflection of the thousands of hours I've spent coaching, helping hundreds of people break free from their limitations, and my own personal growth. Every chapter, every concept, and every piece of advice in this book has been earned through years of dedication, failure, success, and relentless pursuit of understanding how the mind and this world really works.

Most of you are here because something in your life isn't working. Maybe you've felt stuck, frustrated, or overwhelmed by circumstances that seem out of your control. Maybe you're searching for more—more purpose, more clarity, more direction. Whatever brought you to these pages, understand this: you are not here by accident. You are ready for something to change. You are ready to see the world and yourself with new eyes. Prepare yourself. You're about to become a student of human nature and life itself.

In this book you will learn why your relationships feel empty and how to build meaningful, long-term connections. You will understand relationship dynamics and why the masculine and feminine energy is present in every relationship in your life. You will see that depression and anxiety are just illusions of the mind. You will see the importance of keeping your word and why it's the foundation of confidence or self doubt. You will see that you are fooling nobody and why your aura alone tells the world what is really happening in your life. You will learn how to embrace the loneliness that comes with growth, how to be more valuable and irreplaceable, how to use your fears as fuel, and why your perspective determines the kind of world you live in. You will understand why most of your decisions come from boredom and why creating a purpose is your responsibility. This is the blueprint for personal transformation—real, lasting change.

This book is not here to comfort you. It's not here to sugarcoat the truth or make you feel good about where you are. It's here to disrupt you. To push you out of your comfort zone and into a space where real growth can happen. You will be challenged. You will be exposed and that's exactly the point. The fact is most people are so stuck to their ways that the last thing they think about changing is themselves. Some of you are going to read these pages and feel defensive. You'll try to resist what's being said because it hits too close to home. You will get offended because the truth will be in conflict with what you want to believe is true. Others of you will try to cherry-pick— agreeing with what feels comfortable, but avoiding the hard parts. You'll keep one foot in your current reality and one foot in the idea of change, never fully committing to either. Some will read a chapter or two, feel a spark of motivation, and then go right back to their old ways. They'll tell themselves they're "working on it," but they're not. They're playing it safe. They're staying in their comfort zone because that's where they feel in control.

But for a select few of you, this book will be a wake-up call. It will be the slap in the face you've been looking for. It will push you to confront everything you've avoided, to challenge your perspective, to look at the ways you've been holding yourself back, and to finally take full responsibility for your life. It's for the ones who know deep down that something's off. You've felt it—you can sense that there's more to life than the surface-level existence you've been living. You just haven't been able to put your finger on what it is. You're ready to dive into the mirror of truth and finally see yourself for who you truly are, no filters, no illusions, no distractions. You know you're capable of more, but you haven't been able to break through the fog. This is for you, the version of you that's been waiting to wake up. Your mind is about to expand and once the mind is open, it will never go back. Are you ready?

Now, let's begin.

1

PERSPECTIVE
THE WORLD IS IN YOUR HEAD

"With a change in perspective you can instantly turn what you thought was the 'worst' thing to ever happen to you into the 'best' thing to ever happen to you. It all comes down to what you decide to give your attention to."

The world you see is not the world as it is—it's the world through your eyes, your beliefs, and your emotions. Your life is shaped by the lens through which you interpret reality. There's the objective truth "what is", and then there's *your* perspective of it. Your perspective, formed by years of conditioning, personal experiences, and emotional patterns, determines what you focus on, what you ignore, and how you feel about it all. Life becomes the angle through which we choose to see it.

How you feel about yourself, and what you believe you are capable of will dictate your decisions, your opportunities, and what you believe is possible. The way you perceive yourself creates a self-fulfilling prophecy. When you hold a belief that something is impossible, you stop yourself from even attempting it. Your mind has already decided the outcome, so you don't take the necessary actions to make it happen. You avoid the challenge, tell yourself it's not worth the effort, or rationalize why it won't work out. In doing so, you ensure that the outcome aligns with your belief.

How many opportunities have you missed simply because you didn't believe they were possible for you? How many times have you settled for less, not because you were incapable of achieving more, but because you convinced yourself it wasn't possible? This is the power of the mind —both to limit you and to free you. The moment you believe something is beyond your reach, you create a reality where that belief becomes true.

You are the problem and you are the solution.

The power to transform your life is already inside you, and it starts with your mind. Every struggle you face, every setback, every perceived limitation has roots within you. It means that you have the ability to influence, to change, and to overcome any obstacle. The world will always present challenges, but the way you experience those challenges, the way you respond to them, and the outcomes you achieve are shaped entirely by your mind.

Most people walk through life reacting to everything that comes their way, thinking that their problems exist outside of them. They blame other people, unlucky moments, or their environment for why things aren't going their way. This mindset keeps them trapped in the role of a victim, forever looking for solutions outside of themselves, hoping that the next opportunity or the next big break will finally change their life. But this is a false hope because the real solution lies within.

When you accept that you are the problem, it's not about self-blame or guilt. It's about radical responsibility. It's about acknowledging that your beliefs, your patterns, your fears, and your doubts are the real obstacles standing in the way of your success. And once you recognize that, you can stop waiting for the world to change and start changing yourself. If you are the problem, that also means you are the solution. The same mind that created the limitations you face is the mind that can dissolve them. The same beliefs that are holding you back can be reshaped to propel you forward. Transformation starts with a shift in perspective, a conscious decision to stop seeing the world as something happening *to* you and instead, recognizing that the world is responding to the way *you* are thinking and acting. We are all getting the results we deserve.

Changing your perspective, changes the experience.

A change in perspective isn't just a feel-good, motivational concept—it's the answer to every problem you face. Your mind doesn't just perceive the world; it actively shapes your experience of it. Every problem you think you have is filtered through the lens of your perspective. Your mind creates both the problems and the paths to overcome them. The obstacles you face aren't objective truths—they are perceptions, conclusions that your mind has drawn based on the way you see yourself and the world around you.

If you think you've lost, you've already lost. That's not just a metaphor—it's a fact. Your mind will begin to find evidence to support whatever belief you've accepted as true. If you believe you're defeated, your brain will look for proof of that defeat in everything you encounter. It will shape your actions, your body language, and your decisions in ways that reinforce that belief. The opportunity for success could be staring you in the face, but you won't see it because your mind has already decided it's impossible.

On the other hand, if you shift your perspective—if you start to believe that a solution exists, that success is possible—your mind will work just as hard to find evidence for *that* belief. It's not magic; it's the way your brain works. What you focus on, you amplify. Your mind is constantly scanning your environment, filtering information, and interpreting it based on your belief system. When you believe something is possible, your brain becomes a tool for finding solutions, seeing opportunities, and creating pathways forward.

This is why perspective is so powerful. It's not that the world changes when you change your mind; it's that *you* change. The way you engage with the world shifts. You start to see possibilities where before there were only roadblocks. You start to approach problems with curiosity and creativity instead of frustration and defeat. Your entire experience of life transforms because you are no longer trapped by the limits you've placed on yourself.

You are living the results of your philosophy.

What is your religion? Let's be clear—I'm not just talking about traditional faiths. Your religion is the philosophy by which you live, the belief system you hold on to, your number one priority, your guiding force. It's the lens through which you filter every experience, make every decision, and form every belief about what is possible for you. Most people walk through life unaware of what drives them. They act out of habit, react from fear, and follow patterns without ever questioning why they do what they do or what it serves.

Your *religion* is something you might not even realize you have. It's the unconscious set of rules you live by and the unspoken commitments you've made to yourself. For some, their religion is self-doubt. For others, it's avoidance, comfort, or survival. Whatever it is, it dictates every aspect of your life. It controls your choices, your relationships, your ambitions, and even how you handle adversity.

You are living the results of how you see yourself and the world. If you're feeling stuck, overwhelmed, or unfulfilled, it's not because of what's happening around you—it's because of the way you've been approaching life. If you want your life to change, you must change your psychological priorities. This means a shift in focus and respect for your most valuable asset: *your attention*. Where you place your attention, energy, and time determines the course of your life. Your attention is the gateway to your experiences—it dictates what you see, how you interpret events, and how you feel.

Think of your attention like a magnifying glass, wherever you focus it, you'll magnify that aspect of life. If you're focusing on negativity, you're going to see negativity. You'll start to feel like the world is built for you to lose, people are against you, and nothing ever goes your way. And here's the weird part: some people not only experience this negativity, but they also embody it. They live in it, they breathe it, and they make it part of their identity. Why? It sounds crazy but for many, negativity provides comfort. It gives them a sense of purpose, a reason to exist, a way to feel something—anything—because it keeps them in a familiar zone.

Negativity, for some, becomes a form of validation. It's a way to be seen, heard, and acknowledged. The world may be against them, but at least they're the victim in the story. At least they have a role to play, and for some, that role feels safer than facing the unknown. Negativity, in this sense, becomes a shield. It protects people from the pain of trying and possibly not succeeding, from confronting their own potential and the responsibility that comes with it. As long as they stay in that negative space, they don't have to challenge themselves, and they don't have to face the discomfort of growth. It's easier to complain, to focus on what's wrong, and to live in the safety of dissatisfaction than to risk going after what they truly want and discovering that they might fail—or worse, discovering that success requires more than they've been willing to give.

All of this is by choice. No one is doomed to live this way. People choose to stay there because it's familiar, it's comfortable, it doesn't require them to change, it's predictable and that's what makes it so dangerous—it feels safe. But safety doesn't equal happiness, and it definitely doesn't lead to fulfillment. Every action you take, every belief you hold, and every conclusion you've drawn about yourself and the world is influencing your future. It's easy to fall into the comfort of believing that life is happening *to* you, that you're just a victim of circumstances. But that mindset makes you passive, waiting for life to change instead of realizing that you are the one who needs to change. The truth is, life is happening for you and what happens for you happens because of you.

You are the influencer of the end result and regardless of what happens, you have full control over how you react and respond to whatever comes your way. The way you respond is a reflection of who you really are. If you're living in fear, your responses will be defensive, hesitant, and rooted in self-protection. If you're living in self-respect, your responses will be proactive, creative, and solution-focused. Your *religion* determines everything—from your relationships to your career, your health, and your sense of purpose. It's the foundation upon which your entire life is built. Once you understand the truth that your problems are your creation, you hold the key to solving them. You are your only limitation. The world isn't out to get you. It's simply reflecting back the perspective you've chosen to live by. If you want to change your life, change your philosophy.

2

CURIOSITY

UNDERSTANDING THE ROOT CAUSE

"Life will be: What you settle for, what you prioritize, what you give your attention to, and the level of personal responsibility you are willing to take."

Y ou must adopt the mindset of a lifelong student— a student of life itself. This means accepting that the journey of growth and learning never ends. Every experience, every challenge, every victory, and every failure holds lessons that can shape and elevate you. The moment you think you've *arrived* or have nothing left to learn is the moment you start to psychologically decline.

You must approach everything with the mindset that there's always more to uncover, more to understand, more to master. Whether it's about your own psychology, your relationships, or the world around you, life is constantly trying to teach you something. Every experience, good or bad, contains something valuable; you must learn to see the gems hidden within your experiences, within every moment. This means developing a deep understanding of what's for you and what isn't. It's not enough to coast through life, hoping things will magically align in your favor. You have to become curious. You have to become a student of your own problems, your own challenges, and your own situation. The goal is to understand the process of the problem.

Most people treat problems like inconveniences or things to avoid. But the fact is your problems are the key to your growth. Your obstacles are your opportunities. When you take the time to understand the problem, you open up a whole new level of insight. Problems aren't just random occurrences; they are patterns, signals, and feedback loops designed to teach you something critical about your current state of being, your decisions, and your mindset.

Understanding the process of the problem means dissecting it. Instead of focusing solely on the immediate discomfort or frustration a problem brings, you need to step back and look at it from a broader perspective. Ask yourself:

- Where did this problem come from?
- What patterns or behaviors contributed to it?
- What assumptions or beliefs might be fueling it?
- How am I reacting to this situation, and what does that say about me?

When you understand a problem at this level, you begin to see that the solution is embedded within the problem itself. The problem contains the clues and insights needed to overcome it, but you can't see that if you're quick to avoid it. You must first understand it. This is where most people fail—they treat problems like annoyances to get past rather than valuable information to learn from. The problems you face are not random—they are custom-tailored to you, to your current level of understanding, and to the areas where you need to grow. Life doesn't throw meaningless challenges at you. If you're facing a recurring problem, it's because there's a lesson you haven't fully grasped yet. That lesson, once learned, is what will allow you to move forward. As long as you're alive, as long as you're breathing, there's more to learn, more to discover, more ways to grow.

Curiosity leads to clarity. Even if you are unaware and don't understand it now, you are actually where you're supposed to be. The truth is in the details of the position you are currently in. Study you.

Do you even care? Do you have a genuine interest in understanding the problems you're facing right now? Do you care enough to go deep? If you're not fully invested in understanding your situation, you're going to miss the answers staring you in the face. You'll overlook the details, ignore the clues, and remain stuck in the same cycle, wondering why things aren't changing. It's easy to say you want things to be different, but if you're not actively curious—if you're not questioning, researching, and observing—then you're just going through the motions.

Transformation only happens when you become interested in the *why* behind your current reality. Do you know why you are in the position you're in right now? What about you is creating these results? These are the kinds of questions you need to ask yourself every single day. But asking isn't enough. You have to care about the answers. When you care, you inquire. You don't just skim the surface, you go deep. You research, you observe your patterns, your actions, and your decisions. You start to look at your life like a detective trying to solve a mystery. What's causing these results? What's the root of the problem? How can I approach this differently?

When you become genuinely interested, opportunities start to show up. Suddenly, the things you've been over-looking, the details you've been ignoring, become crystal clear. The solutions to your problems don't appear out of nowhere. They've been there all along, waiting for you to see them. But the only way to unlock those doors is by becoming curious enough to knock.

And here's the key: *You cannot fake this.* You can't pretend to care. You can't go through the motions and expect results. I also can't teach you to care. Real change demands real interest. It demands that you invest your energy into truly understanding why you are where you are and what you need to do to move forward.

Most people don't change because they don't care enough. It's really that simple. They might say they want different results, but deep down, they haven't cultivated that hunger to understand their own role in creating those results. They ignore the signs, brush aside the details, and wait for something external to shift. But nothing outside of you will change until you change the way you see and engage with your problems.

You have to care enough to dig deep, to question your own behaviors, your own beliefs, and your own patterns. If you don't care, if you're not interested, nothing will change. You'll stay in the same place, repeating the same mistakes, getting the same results. But the moment you become a student of your own life, the moment you start asking the right questions, everything shifts.

This is the foundation of change. Once you start caring

enough to investigate your own life, to see your problems not as obstacles but as keys to your growth, you'll begin to see solutions everywhere. The answers are waiting for you —but you have to be a student of the game to see them.

3

ALL LOVE
LOVE IS A STATE OF BEING

*"What you are willing to accept is a
reflection of how you feel about yourself."*

Love is a state of being not just a feeling or an
emotion—it's a way of existing, a way of moving
through the world. It's deeper than attraction,
affection, or a fleeting sense of happiness. Love is the core
of who you are, influencing everything you do, every decision you make, and how you see the world around you. It's
internal, constant, and not dependent on outside circumstances or external validation. You don't fall in and out of
it; it's the foundation from which you live.

When love is who you are, you move through life with
intention. You make decisions that align with what's best
for you and reflect your highest values because you understand that loving yourself means choosing what nourishes
your mind, body, and soul. You start to become more selective with your time, your energy, and the people you allow

into your life. You hold yourself to a higher standard, not out of arrogance, but because you respect yourself too much to settle for anything less.

You move with this calm and stable emotional state even in the face of adversity. Love allows you to navigate challenges with grace and resilience because you're not reacting out of fear, anger, or insecurity. Your emotions are balanced, and you're able to respond to life's ups and downs with a sense of calmness and centeredness. It doesn't mean you won't feel anger, sadness, or frustration because you will, but those emotions don't define you or dictate your actions. You can experience them without losing your sense of self. You know they're temporary, passing feelings, but love is permanent. It grounds you and you're able to remain calm and composed in the face of chaos because your inner world is solid.

Living in a state of love pushes you to evolve, to become better, to stretch beyond your comfort zone. It's not about complacency or staying where you are—love, when it's a state of being, drives you to reach your full potential. You refuse to settle for mediocrity because you know you deserve more. This love isn't about accepting yourself as you are, it's about wanting the best for yourself and actively pursuing it. You become your own biggest supporter, pushing yourself to grow, improve, and reach higher because you know that's what true self-love looks like. This is also reflected in how you connect with others. You no longer feel the need to hate on others because you understand that your worth isn't tied to anyone else's success or failure. You support others because you're secure in who you are.

This love is truly unconditional. It doesn't change based on circumstances. You love yourself through your mistakes, your flaws, and your failures, understanding that none of these diminish your worth. You don't withhold love from yourself when things go wrong, and you don't abandon yourself when life gets hard. You remain committed to nurturing that love because you understand it's the foundation of everything else. Without this core, this essence of self-love, everything else begins to crumble.

High standards protect you from low quality experiences.

Self-respect is the deep understanding and acknowledgment that your time, energy, and presence is valuable. When you know your value, you become *slicey*. You start to *slice* through life and move through it differently. When you live with self-respect, you become uncompromising about your values. You know what you stand for, and you don't bend to fit into anyone else's expectations. You're not swayed by popular opinion, peer pressure, or societal trends. You stay true to who you are because you respect yourself enough to live authentically.

It's about making choices that reflect your values, your worth, and your vision for your life. It's about saying *no* to what doesn't serve you and *yes* to what empowers you. It's about honoring your potential, not settling for less, and living with the conviction that you deserve the best. You understand that every detail matters. How you spend your time, the people you choose to surround yourself with, and the moves you make when no one is watching all reflect how much you respect yourself.

Who you are when you are alone is who you are. Do you cut corners when no one is there to hold you accountable? Do you slip into habits that hurt your growth because it's easier? Or do you hold yourself to a higher standard because you know you are watching? Because you know you are responsible for your life? It's in the small, seemingly insignificant moments where your character is truly built.

When you respect yourself, you don't settle. You don't associate with things or people that go against your core values. Your values aren't just something you talk about—they're the standard by which you live by. You live by those values not to impress anyone or to gain approval, but because you know that's what you deserve. You do what is healthiest for you because that's what those who respect themselves do.

**Every problem in your life starts
with not valuing yourself enough.**

The way you talk to yourself is a direct reflection of how much respect you have for who you are. These conversations are more than just the thoughts that run through your mind—they're the ongoing internal dialogue that shapes how you perceive the world, yourself, and your place in it. Every thought, every reaction, every judgment or analysis is part of a larger dialogue. The conversations you have with yourself are incredibly powerful because they shape your mindset, your emotions, and your behavior. What you tell yourself determines how you feel and how you act. You are convincing yourself of something.

You must be your own biggest fan. No one else is going to build you up the way you can. Positive self-talk isn't just about giving yourself compliments; it's about speaking to yourself in a way that reinforces your worth, your potential, and your commitment to growth. You are the person who will push yourself forward or hold yourself back. The dialogue you have with yourself is the foundation of that.

**Focus on love itself instead of loving
the idea of other people loving you.**

When you truly love yourself, it's impossible to hide. It radiates from you. People can feel your confidence, your sense of purpose, and your strength. This energy is contagious—it impacts every room you walk into and every relationship you have. It's in your posture, your tone of voice, and your presence. It's in the way you carry yourself, how you handle challenges, and how you interact with others. People can feel your energy the moment you walk into a room. When you love yourself, you exude a quiet strength and a calm confidence. You're not seeking approval or validation from anyone because you already have it from yourself. That kind of energy is magnetic. People are naturally drawn to it because it reflects a level of self-assuredness that's rare. When someone truly loves and respects themselves, they don't rely on external forces to define their worth, and that creates a powerful ripple effect on everyone around them.

Your self-respect will challenge people to raise their own standards, to respect themselves more, and to interact with the world from a place of true strength. When you don't respect yourself, it shows. It's in the way you carry yourself, in the lack of confidence in your voice, in the way you interact with others—whether through seeking constant validation or shrinking in the face of confrontation. People sense when you're unsure of yourself or when you're acting like someone you're not. This energy can be uncomfortable and even repelling, as it communicates that you're not solid on who you are. You can't hide, we can all see you. When you don't love yourself, people will either unconsciously take advantage of that insecurity or reflect it back to you through their actions. Relationships become transactional, boundaries get blurred, and you start accepting low quality treatment full of disrespect. Remember this: *People will treat you the way you treat yourself.* Your energy sets the tone for how others perceive and interact with you. Building a life on a solid foundation changes how others respond to you, how opportunities present themselves, and how life unfolds around you.

Everything in your life is filtered through how you feel about yourself. If you don't love yourself, if you don't respect yourself, you won't care enough to make the choices that lead to a better life. You'll stay stuck in the same patterns, accepting less than you deserve, because deep down, you won't believe you're worth more. When you build a foundation of self-love, everything changes: you stop settling for mediocrity, you start setting higher standards for yourself and your life. You refuse to accept anything less than what aligns with your worth. Your actions, decisions, and relationships all begin to reflect the love and respect you have for who you are. You create a life that is a true expression of your value and a life filled with purpose, growth, and fulfillment.

This is the foundation of everything. You cannot truly grow without it. You must ask yourself: *Do I love myself enough to do what is best for me? Do I respect myself enough to live by my core values? Or am I settling, self-sabotaging, and accepting less than I deserve?* Every action you take, every decision you make, is either pulling you closer to who you want to become or it's dragging you further away. And if you don't love yourself, you'll never want what's truly best for you. You'll settle for less. You'll accept mediocrity, allow bad habits to persist, and make decisions that sabotage your future for the sake of temporary comfort and pleasure. Loving yourself is the key to everything.

4

MOUNTAIN OF PURPOSE

THERE IS NO HIGH BETTER THAN CLARITY

"Nothing uses up your energy more than waking up with no direction. When there is nothing that fully consumes you, life becomes an endless search for temporary pleasure."

W hat is your vision? This is the question that sets everything in motion. Without a clear vision, you're simply drifting through life, reacting to whatever comes your way with no sense of direction or purpose. Your vision is the compass that guides you, the thing that gives meaning to your actions and decisions. It's not just about what you want to achieve in this world, like wealth, success, or recognition; it's about who you want to *become* in the process. What does that future version of yourself look like? How do they carry themselves? What values do they live by, day in and day out? This vision isn't stamped—it evolves as you grow. But at its core, your vision is rooted in character, values, and purpose. The clearer and more defined your vision is, the more meaningful your decisions will be.

The mountain of purpose is a metaphor for your journey through life, and the climb represents your continuous pursuit of becoming the best version of yourself. Everything on the mountain of purpose is connected. When you think about life as a mountain, it forces you to recognize that every step matters. Every move you make in life is either helping you climb that mountain or pulling you further away from the peak. Every small action, every conversation, every habit, every decision—it all matters.

You can't afford to move mindlessly or act without intention. Some parts of the journey will be steep, filled with obstacles that seem insurmountable. Other times, the path will flatten, giving you moments of rest and reflection. But no matter what, every moment is an important moment—the *now* must be valued and respected. The mountain forces you to confront your limits, your fears, and your doubts. It challenges you to rise above your comfort zone, to push yourself further than you thought was possible.

Each stage of the climb transforms you, shaping your character and your values. Every obstacle is a test of your commitment to your vision. The summit represents the highest version of yourself, but the climb is what prepares you for that peak. The experiences, both good and bad, are what build the strength, wisdom, and perspective you'll need to reach the top. On this mountain, you are not just visualizing who you want to be; you are actively creating it.

**Assets give you leverage, liabilities
keep you struggling—recognize the difference.**

You must identify what is an asset and what is a liability in your life. Not just in terms of money or material possessions, but in terms of people, habits, thoughts, and behaviors. The climb up the mountain of purpose requires clarity about what's helping you rise and what's pulling you down. An asset is anything that builds you, strengthens you, and pushes you forward. It's anything that fuels your growth, supports your vision, tells you the truth, and aligns with the person you are striving to become.

A liability is the opposite—it's anything that slows you down, holds you back, or causes you to fall off the path. It's the negative influences, the unhealthy relationships, the bad habits, and the self-limiting thoughts that chip away at your confidence, disrupt your focus, and pull you further from your goals. They are the excuses, the procrastination, and the poor decisions that lead to regret.

An asset can be people who believe in you and challenge you to be better, or the consistency and discipline that at times can feel repetitive and redundant. It's your daily habits that build momentum, your physical health that fuels your energy, and your ability to stay mindful and self-aware so you can adjust when needed. Learning and continuously growing is a key asset, as knowledge sharpens your skills and broadens your perspective. Love and self-respect will keep you pushing through setbacks, while your vision and purpose act as the compass guiding your decisions. Managing your time effectively, holding yourself accountable, and using creativity to solve problems are also essential assets that help you overcome challenges. Gratitude will fuel your journey, allowing yourself to see progress and remain inspired even when the climb feels tough.

People are a big part of your asset base because the

company you keep directly influences the person you become. The energy, mindset, and habits of those around you rub off on you, whether you realize it or not. If you surround yourself with people who are driven, focused, and committed to their own growth, that energy pushes you to elevate your own standards. On the flip side, if you're surrounded by people who are stuck in mediocrity, negativity, or excuses, it's only a matter of time before their mindset infects yours.

Identifying your liabilities is one of the most important things you can ever do for yourself. These are the behaviors, people, thoughts, and habits that don't just hold you back, they actively drag you down. Liabilities are the things that keep you stuck in place while giving you the illusion of comfort or security. They might feel familiar or safe, but they're secretly keeping you from climbing higher.

A liability can be a relationship that drains your energy —someone who distracts you, creates unnecessary problems, or pulls you into negative cycles. It could be habits like procrastination, laziness, or overindulgence in things that don't add value to your life. These habits might provide short-term pleasure, but they cost you long-term progress, robbing you of the time, focus, and energy needed to grow.

Even more dangerous are the mental liabilities— thought patterns like self-doubt, fear, or insecurity. These thoughts create a ceiling for your growth, convincing you that you're not capable, that you should settle, or that the risks aren't worth taking. This will keep you trapped in mediocrity. Liabilities can also show up as the excuses you rely on when things get tough—the rationalizations you use to avoid discomfort or failure. These are the thoughts and justifications that keep you in your comfort zone, convincing you that staying where you are is good enough.

But in truth, they are what's keeping you from making the leap to the next level.

You have to be willing to look at every aspect of your life and ask: "is this helping me climb?", or "is this weighing me down?" If it's not moving you forward, it's a liability. And once you identify these liabilities, you have to make the tough choice to cut them out. One of the hardest parts of the climb is recognizing when what was once an asset has now become a liability. It takes courage to let go of what you've outgrown, especially if it's been a part of your life for a long time. This is where many people struggle—they hold on to their liabilities because they provide comfort, even though they sabotage progress.

But when you are serious and your vision of the best version of you is clear, you become ruthless in removing anything that hinders your growth. You no longer tolerate the behaviors, thoughts, or influences that keep you stuck. You're willing to sacrifice short-term pleasure for long-term growth because you know that liabilities, if ignored, will stop you from becoming who you're meant to be. You have to cut ties with what doesn't serve your growth, whether it's a wack relationship, a bad habit, or a limiting belief. Otherwise, you'll be carrying dead weight up the mountain, and eventually, it will drag you down or worse, you turn back to fit in with those who've already quit on themselves.

As you move forward in your climb, constantly assess what is an asset and what is a liability. This process is never ending. As you grow, what was once an asset might become a liability, and new assets will emerge as you evolve. Everything in your life either moves you closer to your vision or takes you further away from it. When you understand this, you make decisions with intention. You become selective about where you invest your time, your energy, and your focus. You don't allow liabilities to pull you back down the mountain.

You want to have a great future?
Live a great present. The future is now.

Embody the energy of the person you want to become. This isn't about faking confidence or pretending to be someone else—it's about stepping into that version of yourself right now, in every moment. It's about understanding that who you want to be isn't some far-off goal that you'll reach someday, but a reality you can begin living today. You must fully immerse yourself in the energy, habits, and mindset of the person standing at the summit of your life, because the climb begins the moment you decide to live as that person now.

This means adopting the walk, the talk, the wardrobe, the posture, and the mindset of that future self. You live and breathe this energy in every interaction, every challenge, and every opportunity. Whether you're showing up at work, with your friends, with your family, or in solitude —everything is informed by this vision of who you are becoming. How would this person handle adversity? How would they move through the world? How would they communicate, solve problems, and treat others? You act as though you're already there, because that's how you begin to become it.

This energy isn't just something you tap into occasionally—it becomes your compass, guiding every decision you make. When you're faced with difficult choices, when doubt or fear creeps in, you ask yourself: *Would the person I'm becoming make this choice? How would they handle this?* And you respond accordingly. Every moment is an opportunity to either move closer to that version of yourself or further away. There's no standing still in this process.

This energy is your standard. It's what holds you accountable to your vision, even when no one else is watching. Whether it's how you manage your time, handle stress, or treat those around you—it's all part of the climb, all part of stepping into the person at the top of the mountain. Again, you're not just visualizing success—you're living it, moment to moment, with every action and choice you make.

The mountain strips you down to your core, revealing who you truly are. It forces you to confront your weaknesses, insecurities, and fears, laying them bare in front of you. There's no room for excuses—just raw, honest self-reflection. It exposes your limits, but it also gives you the opportunity to stretch beyond them, to see how far you can push yourself. The climb challenges your endurance, your patience, and your discipline, revealing whether you have the will to keep moving forward when everything in you wants to quit.

Purpose isn't about crossing a finish line; it's endless. It's not about finally getting somewhere and stopping. It's about waking up every day with intention, always pushing to go further, to be better, and to test your limits. Each peak is just a checkpoint on a continuous journey. True fulfillment comes from knowing there's always more to learn, more to conquer, and more to become. That's what keeps you alive, sharp, and hungry. Each summit isn't just a victory—it's a promise to yourself that there's always a next level, and you're willing to do whatever it takes to reach it.

So, as you climb the mountain of purpose, stay focused on who you want to become and be it now. Keep your vision clear, and let that vision guide your actions.

Embrace the climb, knowing that every step, every challenge, and every setback is part of the process. The purpose isn't just to reach the top—it's to become the person who is capable of getting there. The process is the end result, purpose is found in the climb, and the climb never ends.

5

THE OBSERVER
THE TRUTH IS IN THE DETAILS

"Don't be so quick to agree or disagree with what I say. My words are meant to challenge you. It is up to you to observe, question, and study. Those who are serious will dive into it, others will be quick to react. There is instant action only when the mind sees the truth for itself."

Most people move through life feeling lost, drifting without a real sense of direction or understanding of why things happen the way they do. They wake up every day with confusion, reacting to whatever comes their way, yet feeling disconnected from any true purpose. The decisions they make seem random, and even when they achieve what they thought they wanted, it doesn't feel fulfilling. This confusion stems from a lack of awareness—a failure to see the deeper reasons behind their choices and circumstances.

When you lack awareness, life feels like it's happening to you. You don't see the connections between your actions and the outcomes, between your thoughts and the reality you create. You're constantly reacting, not creating. You chase after goals that aren't truly yours, make decisions based on external pressures, and wonder why things never seem to fall into place. This state of being lost is the result of moving through life without truly understanding yourself or the patterns that shape your experiences.

Living in this reactive state is what is creating anxiety. Always feeling behind and unprepared while your mind is racing, trying to keep up with the next problem, the next challenge, or the next demand. You're constantly pulled in different directions, never feeling like you're in control of your own life. You feel stuck, as though no matter what you do, nothing changes—and that's because you're not seeing the full picture. You're not paying attention to the lessons life is offering you.

We must never trust in what we assume and should always question everything we think we know.

Our assumptions and conclusions both play a significant role in shaping how we view the world, and when handled poorly, they can narrow our perspective, distort reality, and keep us from evolving our understanding. These mental shortcuts help us navigate complex situations quickly, but they come with a cost. Assumptions and conclusions, when unchecked, create blind spots. They limit our ability to see new possibilities, prevent us from questioning our beliefs, and lock us into rigid ways of thinking. We stop looking for answers and instead hold on to what we already believe to be true, whether it's accurate or not.

Over time, these unchecked assumptions and conclusions build walls around our mindset, preventing growth and deeper insight. We begin to operate within the confines of our preconceived notions, not realizing that we've created mental barriers to new information. Rather than being open to new evidence or perspectives, we filter everything through the lens of what we already think we know. This limits our ability to adapt, learn, and see things as they really are. In this way, our assumptions and conclusions become self-fulfilling—they reinforce the very beliefs and patterns that may be holding us back.

Assumptions are beliefs or judgments we form without having all the facts. They are based on incomplete information, past experiences, or personal biases. When you make an assumption, you're filling in the gaps of what you don't know with what you think is true. This can lead you to act on beliefs that might not be accurate, creating misunderstandings or misguided actions.

When you assume something, you stop seeking further evidence. You've already decided what's true, and so you miss opportunities to see things from a different angle or uncover new insights. Assumptions come from a place of discomfort with uncertainty—we're wired to want quick answers, and assumptions offer a false sense of clarity. For example, if someone doesn't respond to your message, you might assume they're ignoring you, but in reality, they may simply be busy or dealing with something personal. Making that assumption leads to unnecessary frustration or anger, all based on an incomplete story.

Conclusions, unlike assumptions, are decisions we make after we believe we've gathered enough information. But here's the danger: many conclusions aren't based on real understanding—they're based on what we *want* to believe is true or what we've accepted as truth without question. People reach conclusions that confirm their existing beliefs, locking themselves into a fixed mindset. This is where conclusions become just as limiting as assumptions.

Conclusions that come from what we want to believe, rather than what's actually true, keep us stuck. We form opinions and judgments, not because we've objectively analyzed the situation, but because they fit into a narrative we're already comfortable with. These kinds of conclusions shut down exploration. Once we've made up our mind, we stop challenging our own thinking.

In a relationship, if your partner seems distant or preoccupied, you might assume they're losing interest or upset with you. Without asking or observing the full context, you might jump to the conclusion that the relationship is in trouble. This assumption can lead to defensive or anxious behavior on your part, creating unnecessary tension. The truth may be entirely different—perhaps they're dealing with stress at work or a personal issue unrelated to the relationship. By allowing assumptions and conclusions to drive your actions, you create problems where none existed, and in the process, you might push your partner away, turning your assumption into a self-fulfilling prophecy.

Conclusions lock you into a fixed mindset. Once you've drawn a conclusion, especially one that aligns with your biases or past experiences, you stop questioning it. You accept it as fact, and it becomes a lens through which you view the world. This is dangerous because it prevents you from seeing new evidence or understanding things from a different perspective. The consequences are real. Misunderstandings develop, opportunities slip by, and relationships suffer, all because you're acting on a distorted version of reality. You're no longer open to learning—you're simply reinforcing what you already think you know. This doesn't just limit your understanding; it limits your potential, your relationships, and your ability to navigate life with clarity and purpose.

To move beyond this state of confusion, you need to stop reacting blindly and start observing your life with intention. This is where the power of becoming an observer comes in. Being an observer means stepping outside of the chaos and looking at your life with a fresh pair of eyes. It's about creating distance between yourself and the immediate emotions, distractions, and noise that pull you off course. When you become an observer, you're not just caught up in the moment—you're watching how everything unfolds, studying it, and understanding the deeper patterns at play.

Those who listen without reaction, judgement, and conclusion are the most aware.

An observer is someone who is *above it all* and watches without rushing to react. When you're an observer, you aren't driven by your emotions or assumptions, but by a desire to understand the truth. You're not trying to control or manipulate situations to fit your expectations—you're simply allowing life to unfold, and watching carefully as the truth reveals itself.

An observer notices the small details that most people overlook, seeing beyond what's immediately obvious. They are aware of the nuances in body language, the slight changes in tone of voice, the unspoken shifts in energy that reveal more than words ever could. They pick up on the subtle cues that others miss, understanding that these tiny details hold the key to understanding a situation or person. Observers see patterns—whether in their own behavior or in the actions of others—and they recognize that these patterns are not random. They represent deeper truths, repeated lessons, and the root causes of many of life's challenges.

Observation is about patience. In a fast-paced world, most people are quick to jump to conclusions, not because they've figured it all out, but because they're deeply uncomfortable with the uncertainty that comes from not knowing. The discomfort pushes them to rush, to fill in the gaps with assumptions or half-truths, even when their understanding is incomplete or flawed. They seek a sense of control, even if that control is based on a misinterpretation of the situation. It's easier to jump to a quick conclusion than to sit with the unknown.

But an observer operates differently. They understand that acting too quickly leads to mistakes, missed opportunities, or misunderstandings. This patience gives the observer an edge. While others may be scrambling to react, making decisions based on incomplete information, the observer is gathering insight, carefully piecing together a more complete and truthful understanding. In this way, they avoid the common mistakes of those who rush, and instead, they find opportunities that others miss entirely.

This is very important to understand: *This is not about being passive, inactive, or a pushover.* Observing doesn't mean sitting back and doing nothing—it's about being highly aware and strategic. An observer isn't avoiding action; they're delaying reaction until they have a clear understanding. Being an observer means knowing when to move and when to stay still, when to speak and when to listen. It's about acting from a place of strength, not impulsiveness. An observer gathers the facts, takes in the details, and waits for the right moment to act, not out of hesitation, but out of wisdom.

An observer understands that everything is connected. What happens today might not make sense until weeks, months, or even years later. But if you're watching carefully, you'll begin to notice the patterns, the underlying reasons for why things unfold the way they do. You'll see the connections between your thoughts, actions, and results. Life doesn't just happen to you—there's always a reason. When you take a step back and observe, you see these connections more clearly, and with that clarity comes the power to make better choices.

See things as they are.
Never try to alter, recreate, or deny what you see.

Think of your mind like a browser with multiple tabs open. Each tab represents a situation, conversation, or problem you're processing. These tabs don't need constant attention, but they remain active in the background, gathering information as you go through life. Every time you encounter new evidence—a detail you missed earlier, a shift in perspective, or a new piece of insight—those open tabs update with fresh data. It's not about forcing conclusions right away, but allowing things to unfold and reveal themselves over time.

This approach to life is what separates an observer from someone who's constantly reacting. You don't rush to close the tab too soon by jumping to conclusions or making assumptions. Instead, you let it stay open, allowing the full story to develop before you decide how to act. These tabs remain open, like cases in an investigation, waiting for more evidence. You don't have to dwell on them, but they're there, quietly gathering information as life presents new clues. The key is to let things play out naturally, without forcing conclusions too soon. Life has a way of revealing more evidence over time, and by observing instead of reacting, you give yourself the opportunity to see things for what they really are, rather than what your assumptions or emotions might lead you to believe.

This is what it means to live *above it all.* You're not getting tangled in the immediate emotions of every situation or pulled into the drama of life's daily events. Instead, you're watching from a higher perspective, detached enough to see the bigger picture. You become a student of the process, observing the patterns, dynamics, and feedback that life constantly offers. Every situation—whether it's a challenge, a conversation, a failure, or a success—is information meant to help you grow and understand. It's all data for you to study, rather than something to take personally or react to impulsively.

But there comes a time when you need to close a tab. You close it when you've gathered enough information to form a clear, well-rounded understanding of the situation. Once the pieces fit together, and the evidence is solid, you can confidently make a decision or take action. Closing the tab doesn't mean you rushed to judgment; it means you've patiently observed, collected all the necessary data, and now it's time to act or let go.

Knowing when to close a tab is just as important as knowing when to keep it open. You don't want to obsess over it indefinitely or hold onto something that's no longer relevant. Once you've reached clarity, you let that tab go, make your move, and free up mental space for the next set of challenges or opportunities. It's a balance of knowing when to keep observing and when to conclude.

Take nothing personal. Most people are just revealing how they feel about themselves.

Part of being an observer is learning not to take things personally. When you take things personally, you allow every comment, action, or setback to feel like an attack on your identity or self-worth. This makes you reactive and emotionally charged, clouding your judgment and distorting your perspective. Instead of seeing the situation for what it truly is, you interpret it through the lens of your own insecurities, making everything about you. But the truth is, most of the time, what others say or do has more to do with what's going on in their own world than with you. Their reactions, behaviors, and opinions reflect their own struggles and limitations.

As you grow, your evolution will trigger others. People who are used to seeing you a certain way may feel uncomfortable or threatened by your progress. Your growth can act as a mirror, reflecting back to them their own stagnation or fears, which can lead to negative responses. They may criticize or try to pull you back down, not because of anything you've done wrong, but because your transformation forces them to confront their own lack of growth. If you take this personally, you'll let their insecurities and discomfort shape your journey, making you second-guess yourself or fall back into old patterns.

When you become an observer, you stop internalizing other people's reactions as reflections of your worth. You see their behavior as feedback, not as a personal attack. This detachment allows you to maintain clarity and focus on your own path, without being swayed by the emotional reactions of others. You understand that their discomfort is not your responsibility, and you refuse to let it dictate your choices.

Not taking things personally is key to maintaining your growth. It frees you from being controlled by the opinions and judgments of others, and it helps you stay above the noise and drama. You observe, but you don't absorb. You remain focused on the bigger picture, knowing that your journey is yours alone, and that the reactions of others are just part of the process—not obstacles to your progress.

By stepping back and observing rather than reacting, you protect your energy and stay grounded. This gives you the power to continue evolving without being pulled back by those who may not be comfortable with your growth.

Observation is the gateway to clarity and truth.

When you learn to step back and watch without jumping to conclusions, you gain the ability to see things as they truly are, not as your emotions or assumptions would have you believe. If you understand the true cause of a problem, you can fix it. If you spot a pattern in your behavior, you can break it. But this only happens when you're willing to observe, gather evidence, and allow life to reveal itself, rather than reacting impulsively.

Don't rush, don't force, and don't let your assumptions or conclusions close you off from the truth. The answers you seek are always there, but you must be willing to observe long enough to see them. Every moment and every situation offers feedback, and when you take the time to observe, you begin to see the interconnectedness of events and the deeper reasons behind them.

Understand: *when you become the observer, the level of clarity you gain will be overwhelming at first.* When you start to truly observe, you'll see how lost you've been—how many of your choices were made out of confusion, assumption, or reaction. You'll recognize the truth about the people around you—their intentions, their struggles, and their influence on your journey. The moves you've been making and the patterns you've been repeating will come into sharp focus, and it can be hard to face. You'll see the ways you've been holding yourself back, and that realization can hit hard.

This discomfort is necessary. It's the price of awareness

and the key to breaking free from the cycles that have kept you stuck. Once you see the truth, you can no longer hide from it. The clarity you gain will be a wake-up call. It will show you the moves you need to make, the changes you need to embrace, and the relationships you need to reassess. It might feel overwhelming at first, but it's the only path to true growth. In practicing the art of observation, you gain the clarity to make conscious, deliberate choices that align with who you are and who you are becoming. The more you observe, the more you'll find freedom, wisdom, and the ability to shape your life with purpose and intention.

6

---

1 V 1

YOUR FIGHT

"People don't have 'dating' problems or 'business' problems. They have personal problems that reflect in all areas of life."

What is your fight? The fight I'm talking about isn't just about the battles you have with other people—it's about identifying the problems that are right in front of you. It's the obstacle that demands your full attention, the thing that is blocking your growth, and until you face it head-on, you'll continue to feel stuck.

The most interesting thing to me is that most people already know what they need to do, they're just not doing it. If I told you to write down your next five moves, you would know what you need to address and what you have been ignoring. It's rare that people are oblivious to it. If you don't understand what your fight is, you'll find yourself chasing distractions, solving problems that have nothing to do with what's really stopping you from getting to where you want to go.

The real fight is the one you've been avoiding. It's the one that makes you uncomfortable because it requires you to challenge yourself on a deep level—to look at your fears, your insecurities, and the parts of you that resist growth. And that's why people avoid it. Facing the real fight means dealing with hard truths about yourself. It's the decision to stop procrastinating, to stop allowing fear to dictate your actions, to stop indulging in negative self-talk. It's the decision to confront what's really been keeping you stuck— whether it's an insecurity, a fear of failure, or a habit of self-sabotage. It's easier to pretend the problem is something else to stay busy with distractions and avoid looking at the truth.

Until you confront this fight, you won't grow. There's no other way around it. You can spend years avoiding it, hoping it will resolve itself, but it won't. No amount of distraction, avoidance, or denial will make it disappear. People waste years—sometimes their entire lives—avoiding their real fight. They jump from one distraction to the next, thinking that if they just find the right job, the right relationship, the right opportunity, everything will fall into place. But it never does. They end up back where they started, wondering why nothing has changed.

The fight is often something deeply personal. It's the part of you that's scared to take a risk, the part of you that doubts your own worth, the part that settles for mediocrity. But it doesn't always have to be that deep. Sometimes, your fight is as simple as overcoming laziness or neglecting the small, obvious steps that could open doors for you. It's the things you ignore or procrastinate on because they seem insignificant, but they're exactly what's limiting your mobility, slowly creating more problems, or blocking opportunities.

For example, you avoid having difficult conversations

that would clear the air and move things forward. You avoid it because it's uncomfortable, but that avoidance creates more tension and misunderstanding. This is something so simple, but neglecting this creates more unnecessary problems over time. What's the thing that's holding you back from becoming the person you need to be? Identify it and don't avoid it. Because until you face that fight, you'll stay stuck, no matter how many distractions you chase. You either face the fight or you stay exactly where you are—the choice is yours.

7

ALONE
NEVER LONELY

"A lot of your confusion, stagnation, and unnecessary problems come from the fact that you've settled for and associate with the low hanging fruit."

Most people have a losers mentality. They live life on autopilot, going through the motions, content with just getting by. They settle for comfort, for mediocrity, for what's easy and familiar. They follow the path of least resistance because it doesn't force them to confront the discomfort that comes with real progress. They wake up every day and follow the same dull routines, performing the same tasks, and repeating the same patterns that don't push them beyond where they are. They're content with the familiar because it's predictable, easy, and doesn't challenge them to think critically about their choices or question where they're heading. There's no urgency to change or improve because staying the same doesn't require effort.

The average mind lives in a cycle of short-term gratification. They make decisions based on what feels good in the moment rather than what will benefit them in the long run. They avoid the discomfort that comes with planning for the future, investing in themselves, or doing the hard work that leads to lasting change. For them, life is about getting through the day, making it to the weekend, and finding small distractions to numb the dissatisfaction they feel beneath the surface.

This mindset shows up in every part of their life. In their careers, they clock in and out, doing just enough to not get fired but never enough to excel. They settle for jobs that don't fulfill them because the thought of seeking something greater feels too risky or too difficult. They avoid pushing for promotions, asking for more responsibility, or taking on challenges because failure is a possibility, and failure would force them to confront their limitations. So they stay where they are, collecting a paycheck, living for the weekends, and convincing themselves that this is all there is.

In their relationships, they avoid difficult conversations or confrontations. They don't challenge themselves or their partners to grow because that requires vulnerability and effort. Instead, they settle for relationships that don't inspire or push them, staying with people who share their same comfort zones. They avoid the emotional work needed to build deep, meaningful connections, preferring the safety of shallow, easy interactions that don't ask too much of them.

In their health, they choose convenience over discipline. They eat what's quick and easy, avoiding the gym or any physical activity that requires consistent effort. They tell themselves they'll start next week or that they don't have time, all while knowing deep down that their body and mind are deteriorating. But the short-term pleasure of indulging in unhealthy habits always wins out over the long-term benefits of discipline and self-care. They ignore the warning signs, convincing themselves that they can fix things later, without realizing that "later" never comes.

Average people are reactive, not proactive. They don't plan or set goals with intention. They wait for things to happen to them instead of making things happen. They move according to the pressures around them—whether it's financial stress, health issues, or relationship problems —reacting only when things become urgent. They don't take control of their lives because it's easier to let life happen to them. This passive approach leaves them feeling lost and out of control, but they never question the choices that got them there.

Their free time is spent in passive entertainment. Instead of reading, learning, or developing skills, they binge-watch TV shows, mindlessly scroll through social media, or play video games for hours all while living in misery. These activities are designed to distract them from the uncomfortable feeling that their lives aren't moving forward. They live vicariously through others instead of taking action in their own lives.

They seek external validation instead of internal fulfillment. They care more about how they're perceived by others than about how they truly feel about themselves. They live for approval—whether it's from family, friends, or society at large—rather than living for their own internal sense of purpose. Because of this, they make choices based on what's expected of them, not what they truly want. They stay in careers, relationships, and lifestyles that don't fulfill them because it's "normal" or "safe." They never question if they're actually happy or if they're just going through the motions.

Living an average life and having a losers mentality, means never knowing what you're truly capable of. It means avoiding risk and settling for a life that's far less than what you could have achieved. It's a life of regret disguised as contentment. The day-to-day feels fine, but deep down, there's a sense of dissatisfaction—a sense that you were meant for more but never took the steps to pursue it.

Choosing low-quality connections to escape loneliness only deepens your sense of emptiness.

On this path, most people won't be able to relate to you. They've conditioned themselves to not think about long term growth. Like I mentioned earlier, their world is built around familiarity, doing what's easy, and avoiding the discomfort that comes with change. When you start pushing beyond those limits, it disrupts the comfortable reality they've settled into. Your ambition and desire for more will make them uncomfortable because it highlights their own stagnation. You become a mirror reflecting back to them the things they've been avoiding—their fears, their complacency, and their lack of growth.

Instead of celebrating your progress, they might try to downplay it or pull you back to their level. Not because they're malicious, but because your growth is a threat to their comfort. They don't want to confront their own shortcomings, so they try to keep you in the same box they've placed themselves in. They'll question your goals, make you feel like you're "doing too much," or lowkey try to discourage you from taking risks. It's easier for them if you stay the same because then they don't have to feel bad about their own lack of ambition.

This is where loneliness comes in. You'll feel isolated, like you're speaking a different language with the people you once related to, the ones you shared jokes with, and talked casually with—you'll start to notice the gap between your mindsets. The conversations that once felt comfortable will now feel shallow, and the connections that used to fuel you will feel like they're holding you back. You'll start to see how rare it is to find people who truly understand your hunger for a better life.

This is the loneliness that comes with growth. It's a necessary part of the journey, but it's also one of the most difficult. The higher you climb, the fewer people there will be who can keep up with your pace. Some will distance themselves from you because your ambition makes them uncomfortable, while others won't be able to understand your drive. This is the cost of evolution—outgrowing the old to make room for the new. You're leaving behind the mindset of settling, and with it, the people who are content with mediocrity.

This is what makes many people quit on themselves. When the loneliness sets in, when the people they used to rely on for support or validation no longer understand their vision, they start to doubt themselves. They begin to question whether the journey is even worth it. It feels easier to give up and fall back into the crowd than to keep climbing alone. The discomfort of being misunderstood and not having anyone around to encourage them can make people retreat back into mediocrity.

The weight of this loneliness can be heavy. You feel disconnected from the people around you because your priorities are no longer aligned. Again, you're focused on the long-term vision, the next level, the evolution of who you are becoming, while others are content with short-term satisfaction, staying where it's comfortable. This difference in mindset can leave you feeling like an outsider, constantly questioning if you're the one who's out of place. It's the feeling of not having anyone who truly understands.

This makes it tempting to quit, and go back into old patterns, because being part of the crowd feels safer than being out on your own, chasing something bigger. This loneliness breaks people because they think it's a sign they're on the wrong path. They start to believe that growth is supposed to come with support, with validation, with constant reassurance from those around them. But the truth is, this loneliness is part of the process. Most people are not willing to sacrifice comfort for the unknown. They are not willing to keep pushing when everything feels uncertain. That's why they just stay where they are.

Don't get discouraged when the people you care about the most don't want to grow with you. Not everyone was meant to evolve. Instead, they're here to remind you what it looks like if you don't.

You can't win alone. No matter how strong or determined you are, success isn't a solo game. You need a round table—a group of people who will hold you accountable, push you to improve, and offer insight you might not see on your own, but this isn't just about mentors, business partners, or friends who give advice. The round table we're talking about is deeper than that—it's the people, real or imagined, who live in your mind. It's the voices you allow to shape your decisions, the people whose perspectives guide how you live and how you approach your goals.

How would you live if you knew God was watching, guiding you, making sure you win? You'd move with purpose, with focus, knowing that you're not alone in this journey. Every decision would feel meaningful, every step deliberate, because you'd understand that a higher power has your back. This is why God and religion are so powerful. They give people a sense of direction, a sense that their life is part of something bigger. They create an unshakable belief that no matter how hard things get, they are not walking alone.

With this belief, there's no room for doubt. You'd carry yourself differently. You wouldn't hesitate or second-guess your decisions because you'd know that there's a plan for you, that everything is unfolding for a reason. God becomes not just a distant force but an active guide in your life. You'd approach challenges with the mindset that they're designed to build you, not break you, knowing that you're being pushed toward something greater. Whether you believe God is real or not, that guiding energy is very real. The impact is real, which makes God real for those who truly believe.

Your round table should function with this same energy. Think of it like a board of directors for your life. These aren't just random people who give you advice when things get tough; they are the ones who consistently set the standard for how you approach your life, how you solve problems, and how you stay on track. These people represent the qualities you want to cultivate, the mindset you need to adopt, and the discipline that's necessary for you to reach your highest potential.

The round table is made up of the people whose voices have the most influence on your decisions and actions. This could be people you know personally, like mentors, friends, or family members, or it could be people you admire from afar—authors, thought leaders, athletes, entrepreneurs, or even fictional characters. The key is to choose people who represent the standards you hold for yourself and the life you're trying to build.

Think of these people, not as idols, but as partners. They are not above you; they are with you on this journey. What makes them valuable is not their fame or success, but how their mindset and actions align with the person you want to become. If you respect someone's work ethic, discipline, or mindset, ask yourself: What would they do in this situation? How would they approach this problem? Their voice becomes part of your internal dialogue. You consult them, mentally, as a partner in your success—not as a fan admiring from a distance.

Your round table should be composed of individuals who challenge your thinking, who encourage you to go beyond what's comfortable, and who live out the values you're striving to embody. They are there not to make you feel good but to push you to think bigger and work harder. These are the voices you need in your head when you're faced with tough decisions, moments of doubt, or the temptation to settle for less than you're capable of.

Even if you don't have direct access to the people you admire, you can still build a powerful mental core. In your mind, there are no limits to who can sit at your round table. You can pull from books, interviews, documentaries, or speeches—any source that gives you insight into how successful people think and operate. This mental round table is built on the qualities and values you want to live by.

Imagine that every time you're faced with a decision, your round table is there with you. They are there to help you navigate, to remind you of the standard you've set for yourself, and to push you to think about what's truly important. What would they say if they saw you slacking? How would they react if you gave up too soon? These voices guide your actions because they reflect the principles you've chosen to live by.

You have to be deliberate about who you let sit at your table. If the people around you are negative, lazy, or stuck in a cycle of making excuses, their mindset will slowly become yours. You'll find yourself justifying your own lack of progress by comparing yourself to those who aren't moving forward either. That's why you must build a mental round table of winners—people who won't allow you to get comfortable with less than your best.

In the end, your round table isn't just a collection of people, it's a mindset. It's a reminder that you're never really walking the path alone. God is watching and you've got a team, a council of high-achievers, serious thinkers, and inspirational figures who are walking with you, even if only in your mind. You are the average of the voices you listen to, so choose them wisely. Make sure the people at your round table reflect the person you want to become. Let their influence shape your growth, guide your decisions, and hold you to the standard of excellence you know you're capable of achieving. With the right round table, there's no limit to how far you can go.

8

FEAR

SUFFERING FROM IMAGINATION

"Fear only exists in our thoughts of the future. It is our imagination that is causing us to fear what is not here at the moment or what may never exist. This is why most of us are suffering more from imagination than in actuality."

Fear is one of the most powerful forces that controls human behavior. It's embedded in the most primitive parts of our brain—the parts designed to keep us safe from physical harm, danger, or threats. In the early stages of human evolution, this instinct served a critical purpose: it kept us alive. Fear of predators, fear of isolation, fear of the unknown—these were essential for survival. But today, in a world where most of these physical threats are no longer present, fear has adapted. Instead of just keeping us safe from life-threatening dangers, it now protects us from anything that threatens our sense of self, our comfort, or our social standing.

Fear taps into the primal need for acceptance and belonging. The fear of rejection isn't just about someone not liking you—it's about the deep-seated fear of being cast out, of losing your place in the group. In ancient times, being outcast from your tribe could mean death, and that instinct still lingers today. We fear stepping out of line, speaking up, or taking risks because we're wired to avoid anything that could make us an outsider. Fear tricks you into believing that failure or rejection will cost you more than it actually will.

The fear of failure goes beyond simply messing up—it's tied to the fear of losing status, security, and self-worth. Your mind makes you believe that if you fail, it's not just a temporary setback; it's a reflection of your identity, your capability, and your value as a person. This fear stops you from trying new things and taking the risks that could lead to growth. Your survival instinct kicks in, telling you that failure equals danger.

The mind craves certainty and fear thrives in uncertainty. When you can't predict what's going to happen, your mind fills in the gaps with fear-based assumptions. The unknown feels like a threat because your brain can't guarantee safety or success, so it creates a narrative that stepping into the unknown will lead to loss—whether it's the loss of security, comfort, or self-image.

In today's world, fear is no longer about survival in the literal sense, but about protecting the ego, the identity, your beliefs, and the social structure you've built around yourself. The fear of loss—whether it's losing your job, losing respect, or losing control—keeps you locked into patterns of behavior that are safe but stagnant. It makes you believe that the discomfort of stepping into the unknown is more dangerous than the dissatisfaction of staying where you are.

This deep, primal wiring is why fear can feel so overwhelming and inescapable. It taps into your most basic need for security, but in doing so, it holds you back from betting on yourself. Fear convinces you that avoiding risk is the same as avoiding danger, but in actuality, it causes you to miss out on opportunities for growth, success, and transformation.

"Misery" is accepting the position you are in because of the fear you are unwilling to address.

What do you fear? Is it failure? The fear that if you try, you'll fall short? That you'll confirm the doubts you've always had about yourself? That people will say, "*I told you so,*" or that you'll prove your own inner critic right, feeding the belief that you're not capable?

Is it rejection? The fear that if you put yourself out there, people won't accept you, won't understand you, or won't value you? Do you fear being seen, only to be overlooked, dismissed, or criticized? Is it the fear that being vulnerable will expose you to judgment, making you feel like you don't belong?

Is it the unknown? The fear of stepping into something unfamiliar, something you can't predict or control? Do you fear that once you leave your comfort zone, you'll be lost? That the uncertainty will overwhelm you, and you won't be able to handle what comes next? Does the thought of not knowing what's ahead keep you from moving forward?

Is it success? The fear that if you actually achieve what you set out to do, your life will change in ways you're not ready for? That with more success comes more responsibility, more expectations, more pressure? Do you fear that success will force you to rise to a new standard, to maintain it, and that deep down, you're not sure if you can? Are you afraid that success will separate you from the people you know, from the comfort of being *good enough,* and push you into a world where more is demanded of you?

Or is it change? The fear that things will shift, and with that shift, you'll lose the familiar, even if the familiar isn't what you want? Do you fear that once you start changing, you won't recognize your life, or yourself, anymore? Does the idea of losing who you are, even if that person is stuck, hold you back from growth? Look closely at what you fear. Are you afraid of the reality of these things, or the stories you've built around them? Are these fears based on actual threats, or are they projections of what *could* happen, but hasn't yet? How much of your fear is shaped by your past, by assumptions you've made about your limitations, and how much of it is rooted in truth?

Fear is the biggest illusion of them all. The very thing that paralyzes you and stops you from moving forward *doesn't even exist yet*. It only exists in your imagination. Fear tricks you into reacting to something that hasn't occurred, convincing you to act as if the worst outcome is already a fact, but fear itself is not a fact—it's an emotion. It feels real because it comes with a strong emotional response. When you're afraid, your body reacts. Your heart races, your palms sweat, your breathing quickens. These physical sensations trick you into believing that something dangerous is happening right now, even when it's not. Fear hijacks your nervous system, making you think that you're in immediate danger, when all that's really happening is that your mind is imagining a future problem.

All of this is self made. It comes from how you interpret a situation, not from the situation itself. Two people can face the same challenge—one may feel fear, while the other feels excitement or confidence. The difference is in one's perspective. Fear is subjective, built on your personal history, beliefs, the narrative you've created about yourself, how prepared you are, and how you choose to label and respond to uncertainty.

The situation is neutral—it's your mind that assigns meaning, labels it as threatening, and creates the fear response. For one person, uncertainty represents danger—it's a signal that things could go wrong and failure is around the corner. For another person, that same uncertainty represents possibility—it's a chance to grow, to discover something new, to prove themselves in the face of adversity. The external situation doesn't change, but how you choose to frame it does. Which means *why* you fear, is more important than *what* you fear.

Fear only holds power because you haven't fully faced it. It thrives in the gaps where truth hasn't been fully revealed. But the moment you step into that fear and look at it head-on, you realize it was a creation of your mind, a distorted story fueled by doubt, lack of preparation, insecurity, and anticipation of the worst. You can either let fear control you, or you can choose to see it for what it is—an interpretation, a story you've told yourself, and something you have the power to change.

Nothing in life is to be feared, it's only to be understood.

Fear serves as the foundation for many systems and structures. Think about the way laws, insurance companies, security systems, and even social norms are created to protect against worst-case scenarios. These systems are designed to mitigate risk, manage uncertainty, and provide a sense of control. Fear influences everything from how we build our homes to how we interact with one another—entire industries exist because of the fear of potential loss, failure, or harm.

The healthcare industry, the legal system, financial markets—all of these are constructed with fear as a driving force, anticipating what could go wrong and creating protections to prevent it. Governments, businesses, and communities develop rules, plans, and safeguards all based on the need to manage fear. These systems just show the power that fear holds over decision-making.

At its core, fear is meant to keep us safe, to alert us to potential dangers, and to help us navigate the unknown. In moments of real threat, fear sharpens your instincts—it heightens your senses, increases your focus, and prepares your body to act. It's a survival mechanism that's built into your biology, a tool that keeps you alert when true danger is present. Despite being an illusion, fear serves a purpose.

We need fear because it pushes us to pay attention. It warns us when something might be off, when we need to slow down, observe, or reassess. In moments where there's real risk—whether physical, emotional, or mental—fear acts as a guide. It tells you, *"Look closer, proceed with caution,"* and in those moments, it's not about paralyzing you, it's about protecting you from serious harm.

That's why understanding fear is crucial. It challenges you to assess what's real and what's imagined, and when you understand its role, it becomes a tool—not a limitation. Fear, in its proper place, sharpens your awareness, helps you stay grounded, and motivates you to prepare for challenges. It's there to keep you alert, but it's not meant to stop you from doing what is best for you. When you can differentiate between the fear that protects you and the fear that holds you back, you can use it to your advantage. Once you welcome the fear with clarity, preparation, and with understanding, the illusion ends instantly and *"what is"* is used as fuel.

9

BOREDOM

THE WAR AGAINST NOTHING

"Boredom, lack of purpose, lack of direction is dangerous to the mind. The mind is unlimited, it can think and create whatever story it wants. Every story one creates in their mind about the world and themselves can be seen as 'truth' causing all kinds of confusion within oneself."

I n the beginning of time, life was filled with purpose, urgency, and meaning. Every single day presented a challenge that demanded your full attention. The mind had to be alert, alive, and constantly aware of the environment. Survival was the ultimate purpose, and everything revolved around that goal. Imagine living in a tribe, where food wasn't guaranteed and every meal was earned through skill, patience, and focus. You couldn't just go to a store and pick up what you needed. If you didn't hunt, you didn't eat. The tribe would spend days preparing for a hunt—scouting the land, tracking animals, and waiting for the right moment to strike. There was no certainty, no safety net, everything depended on your ability to be alert and connected to the environment.

You had to study animal behavior, understand migration patterns, and learn the land in detail. You had to know where the water sources were, where the animals slept, where they grazed, and where they would flee to if startled. If you wanted to catch an animal, you had to truly understand its habits. You needed to know what time of day it was most vulnerable, how it reacted to different sounds, and what it feared. The slightest miscalculation could mean the difference between eating for the next few days or going hungry. You had to be observant—tracking footprints, studying broken branches, noticing subtle changes in the landscape that indicated where animals had passed. Miss one small detail, and the entire hunt could fail.

This required intense focus, mental sharpness, and a constant awareness of the environment. You weren't just walking through the woods aimlessly—you were scanning for signs of life, tuning into the rhythms of nature, and using every bit of knowledge and skill at your disposal to outsmart your prey. You had to be fully present and fully engaged because your survival depended on it.

Every sound, every shadow, every breeze mattered. You had to be one with the natural world, listening to it, learning from it. There was no room for distractions. The tribe's success, the well-being of your people, and your own life hung in the balance. This wasn't just a task—it was a life-or-death mission. One wrong step could scare the animals, driving them far away, and one missed opportunity could mean days without food.

This way of life demanded mental clarity and sharp instincts. You had to be resourceful, constantly adapting to the environment and learning from every experience. If a trap failed, you needed to figure out why. If the animals moved differently than expected, you had to adjust your strategy. You couldn't rely on luck—you had to rely on your mind's ability to absorb information, make quick decisions, and stay alert to every possibility.

Early humans learned how to manipulate fire, a tool that changed everything. It had to be controlled, nurtured, and mastered. They had to learn how to create it, protect it, and use it to cook food, repel predators, and provide warmth in the night. Fire was essential for survival. Your very existence depended on how well you could manage it. This responsibility demanded full engagement of the mind. If you didn't keep the fire alive, you'd be left cold and vulnerable, especially in the darkness of the night.

Purpose wasn't something you had to search for—it was built into the very fabric of life. Each day, there was something to do. You either hunted, protected, built, gathered, or taught others how to survive. The human mind, in those early days, was alive. Every moment had weight, and every action had meaning. There was no time to be passive, every instinct had to be honed, and every skill sharpened, or else the unforgiving environment would make you pay the price.

Everything in those days had meaning because everything had consequences. In today's world, that urgency has been taken away. The world is no longer as dangerous, and survival doesn't demand the same kind of mental engagement. You don't have to hunt for food, build your shelter, or make fire to stay warm. Technology has made things convenient, and while this convenience has improved our quality of life, it's also numbed our senses. We've lost that primal connection to life's deeper meaning. Our minds, once sharp and alive with purpose, have become sluggish and dull.

An idle mind will hurt itself and create
chaos to make a boring life interesting.

Instead of having to constantly be alert, many people now drift through life on autopilot. There's no urgency, no real threat, no need to be fully present. The mind, which once had to be active for survival, is now idle. The idle mind is a dangerous state of existence. It's not a mind that lacks intelligence, but one that lacks engagement, curiosity, and purpose. It drifts through life without direction, avoiding the discomfort of challenge and the effort required for growth. The idle mind isn't always obvious — many people live with it without even realizing. On the surface, they seem to function normally, going to work, fulfilling their daily responsibilities, and interacting with others. But underneath, the mind is passive, detached, and unchallenged. It avoids deep thinking, avoids pushing boundaries, and avoids anything that requires it to stretch beyond the comfort of routine.

When the mind is dull you wake up, go to work, come home, and repeat, day after day. There's no fire, no drive, no deeper sense of purpose. You exist, but you're not truly living. Your job feels pointless, your relationships feel empty, and the things that once brought you joy now feel like obligations. It's a subtle but overwhelming feeling that nothing you do really matters. The dull mind doesn't seek new information, it doesn't ask questions, and no longer strives for growth.

The mind craves stimulation. When the mind has no meaningful direction, it creates its own distractions. In the absence of real challenges, it will create artificial ones. You'll turn minor inconveniences into sources of frustration, blowing things out of proportion just to have something to focus on. Without direction, the mind invents battles to fight—battles that don't need to be fought—while avoiding the real work that could lead to growth.

Nothing puts more pressure on the human mind than nothing. The idea of having nothing, being nothing, and doing nothing consumes the human mind more than anything else. The mind seeks out noise to drown out the silence of an unfulfilled life. It would rather be occupied with distractions than sit still and face the emptiness that comes from a lack of meaningful pursuit.

A lot of stupid decisions come from being bored, lonely, and horny. Stop investing your time and energy in all the wrong places (with all the wrong people) for a moment of pleasure. Give all of yourself to a vision and create a life you don't have to escape from.

Escapism is the path most people take when they can't confront the reality of their lives. It's what happens when the mind becomes idle, when there's no real purpose, no real drive, no vision pulling you forward. Without deep meaning or purpose, most people's goals in life come down to just one thing: *feeling*. People just want to feel something. They chase sensation, distraction, anything that will make them feel alive for a moment. Instead of building something meaningful, people chase the next quick thrill, the next dopamine hit, the next distraction to fill the void. Escapism becomes a way of life.

In the process of escape, you train your brain to seek out instant gratification rather than long-term growth. The mind becomes conditioned to avoid discomfort and settle for ease, losing its capacity for resilience, focus, and real depth. The more you escape into shallow distractions, the less mental sharpness you have. You no longer push yourself to think deeply, to question, or to challenge yourself.

The mind, once a powerful tool for navigating life, becomes sluggish, passive, and dependent on external stimulation to feel alive.

Again, every time you seek out quick dopamine hits—whether through social media, porn, drugs, or meaningless conversations—you're rewiring your brain to need constant external stimulation. This makes it harder to stay present, to focus on anything that requires sustained effort or patience. You find yourself restless, unable to concentrate, and more easily distracted. By constantly avoiding reality, you never give your brain a chance to work through the issues you're running from.

You're always on edge, always trying to outrun the very issues that would bring you peace if you faced them head-on. The more you indulge in fantasy, the more disconnected you become from the real world. You begin to live in an illusion, a self-created bubble where you believe the world should cater to your desires without effort. This disconnection makes it harder to deal with life's inevitable challenges, as you've trained your mind to expect easy, fast rewards.

When you avoid discomfort at every turn, you lose the ability to embrace difficulty. The mind becomes fragile, weak, unable to handle stress, rejection, or failure. Instead of seeing challenges as opportunities for growth, you start seeing them as threats to avoid. This leaves you unprepared to deal with real life. The longer you run, the more you feel the weight of that avoidance. This creates this weird mental loop where you escape to avoid guilt, but the escape itself makes you feel even worse. Over time, this will spiral into deep frustration and emptiness, as it hits you that you're wasting your potential and settling for far less than you're capable of. The mind becomes trapped in a state of stagnation. It stops evolving, stops growing, and stops seeking out new ideas or challenges. You settle into a routine of distraction and avoidance, living a life that's mentally unfulfilling and disconnected from any real sense of purpose.

When you waste energy on escaping your problems, life (God, the universe) ensures you learn the hard way where focus should've been.

The mind and body are deeply connected, and the effects of escapism don't stop in your head—they manifest physically as well. Constant avoidance of real problems and chasing temporary distractions can lead to physical consequences like hormonal imbalances, chronic fatigue, and other stress-related illnesses. The stress of unresolved issues builds up in your system, weakening your immune response, throwing off your body's natural balance, and leading to a range of physical problems. Your body is always communicating with you, reflecting the state of your mind. Your inability to face life's challenges head on creates a ripple effect in your physical health, causing the body to break down under the weight of unresolved issues and constant escape from reality.

Whether it's the rush of attention from a social media post, the thrill of a new purchase, taking a vacation, or the short-lived high from alcohol or drugs, it all comes down to one thing: avoiding the emptiness that comes with a life lacking in direction. Chasing temporary pleasure keeps you locked in a loop, constantly seeking, but never finding anything of real substance. It's a trap. The void inside never really disappears; it just gets temporarily masked by the next hit of sensation. You're left needing more—more intensity, more distraction, more of whatever keeps you from facing the reality of your situation. In the pursuit of these shallow experiences, you sacrifice real growth and depth. You drift further from the fulfillment that can only come from living with purpose and intention. The relationships are surface-level, the achievements are hollow, and the moments of joy are fleeting. You become trapped in a pattern where nothing ever lasts, and nothing ever satisfies. You end up running from yourself, avoiding the deeper work that needs to be done, chasing things that were never meant to last. The mind, which once thrived on being active, is now deteriorating from lack of use.

The reality is (to wrap this all up) there is no real escape. No amount of distractions can fill the void left by an unfulfilled life. No temporary high can substitute for a sense of purpose. The more you run from your problems, the bigger they become, and the more disconnected you feel from yourself and your true potential. True growth requires you to engage with life, not run from it. It requires you to stop distracting yourself with meaningless activities and start focusing on what really matters. The human mind was never designed to be idle. It was built to solve problems, to learn, to grow, and to constantly evolve. The survival instinct that once kept the mind sharp has faded into the background, leaving a void. People have become disconnected, uninspired, and bored, not because life has nothing to offer, but because they've lost touch with their inherent need to be engaged with it.

The only way to break the cycle of escapism is to confront the truth, to face the discomfort, the fear, and the uncertainty head-on, and to stop seeking temporary relief at the expense of lasting fulfillment. When you live with intention and you have a vision that pulls you forward, there's no need to escape. You're fully engaged, fully alive, and fully committed to the process of becoming the person you're meant to be.

10

LABELS

BLINDED BY SOUNDS & DEFINITIONS

"The easily offended are the easily manipulated. When the mind is that quick to react, when it's that fragile, that easily hurt, one can just feed it comfortable lies and it will just accept."

Words are powerful. They shape how we think, how we feel, and how we perceive the world. But are we seeing reality, or are we seeing the world through the definitions of words? Is it possible that we are lost within language itself? Words are not just sounds; they are symbols that carry meaning, and those meanings create how we feel. Every word comes with its own set of meanings, assumptions, and expectations that we accept without question. The way we label things—people, emotions, experiences—creates a framework for how we understand them. But this framework can be limiting. Instead of observing a situation or emotion for what it truly is, we filter it through the lens of language, through the meaning we've been taught to attach to those words.

The more words we know, the more we think we understand. But is that really true? Words give us a way to communicate ideas, but they also create boundaries around those ideas. If someone doesn't understand the language I speak, to them my words are meaningless—just sounds with no inherent value or understanding attached. So, do we think in sounds and definitions? Are we trapped in the words we've learned, using them as a substitute for direct experience? And if we are, are we really seeing the world as it is, or are we seeing it through the filter of language?

If someone insults you, it's not the sound of the word that hurts—it's the meaning behind it, the definition you've accepted. But why does it bother you so much? Is it the word itself that holds power over you, or is it because there's something within you that remains unresolved? The truth lies in understanding why it bothers you. You get offended by words, but what is that revealing about you?

Words are neutral until we assign them meaning. If someone calls you a loser, it's not the word that causes pain—it's your relationship to that word. It's the fear or insecurity you have about being a loser that causes the sting. The insult digs into the areas of your life that you're unsure about, the parts of you that you haven't fully addressed. But here's the real question: If you didn't believe there was some truth to the insult, would it still bother you?

When you react strongly to a word, it's a signal that something deeper is at play. It's not just the label that hurts—it's the fact that, on some level, you've accepted that label as a possibility. You've given it power over you because there's a part of you that hasn't been fully understood, accepted, or confronted. The word exposes your insecurities, your fears, and your doubts.

But there's another layer to this—who the words come from. If the same insult was said to you by a stranger on the street, would it hit as hard as when it comes from someone you care about or respect? Caring who it comes from plays a huge part in why you take it personally. When someone close to you, someone whose opinion matters, says something hurtful, it feels like an attack, not just on the surface, but to your core. You value their perspective, and when they say something that hits a sore spot, it's harder to dismiss. You take it to heart because it feels more like a truth you've been avoiding rather than just empty words.

Whether the words come from a stranger or someone you care about, it's your reaction to them that determines their impact. The insult, the judgment, the criticism—they all reflect something within you, not just the intent of the person saying them. Why does their opinion matter so much? Why do their words hold so much weight? It's not the word that's the problem—it's what the word reveals about you. It's a reflection of your inner world, a mirror showing you the areas where you still need to grow, to understand, and to heal.

Labels help us categorize and understand the world. They provide structure and allow us to navigate life by simplifying complex ideas, people, and situations. Labels are shortcuts—ways for the brain to process information quickly and make sense of all the experiences we encounter. Without labels, we would struggle to make distinctions, to define roles, or to recognize patterns. Labels help us create a sense of order in what could otherwise be overwhelming chaos. We use labels to identify ourselves, to describe others, to form relationships, and to create structure in society. They're a natural part of how we think, helping us make snap judgments and understand the world at a glance.

But here's the problem with labels: *they limit us.* While they help us categorize, they also box us in. When we label ourselves or others, we reduce something that is ever-changing to a fixed definition. It's convenient, yes, but it's also restrictive. Instead of seeing a person or a situation for the complexity it holds, we settle for a simplified version of the truth—one that fits within the confines of the label we've assigned. We start to live within the boundaries of those labels, losing sight of the fact that people and situations are constantly evolving.

A human mind is so powerful. We can invent, create, experience, and destroy things with thoughts alone.

Imagine being diagnosed with anxiety or depression. The moment you hear the diagnosis, a label is applied. You understand the definition. You internalize it. You identify with it. From then on, your thoughts and actions are filtered through the definition of that label. You might start saying, *I am anxious*, or *I have depression*, and suddenly your identity shifts. You begin to act in ways that align with the definition of anxiety or depression, limiting yourself to the confines of that label. The label becomes your reality.

But what is anxiety, really? What is depression? We throw these terms around so often that they've become part of our everyday vocabulary, but do we truly understand what they mean? Do we understand the process of this problem, or have we simply accepted the label as our identity? When someone says, *I have anxiety* or *I'm depressed*, what they mean is that they feel overwhelmed, lost, or stuck. But the moment we slap a label on it, we stop digging deeper. We stop questioning what's really happening beneath the surface. What if anxiety is not something you "have" but rather a temporary state of being? Anxiety is often described as a feeling of worry, nervousness, or unease about something with an uncertain outcome. But is it really something you "have" like a possession, or is it simply a reaction to your current circumstances? What if anxiety is just your mind's way of responding to uncertainty or a lack of clarity? What if it's a signal telling you that something in your life needs attention, change, or understanding?

When you slap a label on it—*I have anxiety*—you make it permanent in your mind, something fixed, something you believe you're stuck with. You create a narrative where anxiety becomes part of your identity, rather than seeing it as a passing emotion or a response to a temporary situation. Without the label, you can start to observe what's actually happening in your body and mind. You feel your heart racing, your hands shaking, your breath quickening. These are just symptoms—your body's natural response to fear or uncertainty. But by calling it *anxiety*, you begin to identify with the feeling, rather than seeing it as a temporary state. When you see the symptoms for what they are— a racing heart, a tense body, shallow breathing—without attaching the label of anxiety, you give yourself the chance to address the root cause. You ask, *Why is my heart racing? What am I afraid of right now? What am I avoiding or uncertain about?* Changing your perspective, changes the experience. Now you can take action to change the situation instead of accepting the label and allowing it to dictate your life.

The same goes for depression. What if depression is not a permanent condition but a reflection of where you are in life at a given moment? Depression is often linked to feelings of hopelessness, sadness, or disconnection. But what if those feelings are not who you are but rather a reflection of your current state—your environment, your mindset, your actions, or your relationships?

By labeling yourself as *depressed*, you lock yourself into a cycle of thinking that tells you this is just the way it is, instead of seeing it as a signal that something in your life needs to change. Depression could be your body's response to unmet needs, unresolved issues, or a life out of alignment with your true desires. Without the label, you can see the symptoms more clearly. You might notice a lack of energy, a feeling of heaviness, or a desire to withdraw from others. These are signs—messages from your body and mind—that something is out of balance. When you see these symptoms without the label, you can start to address the underlying issues. You ask, *"Why do I feel so disconnected?"* *"What am I not addressing in my life?"* *"What needs are not being met?"* Without the label of depression, you're not trapped in the idea that you're powerless or stuck. You start to see that these feelings are responses, not permanent conditions.

The moment you accept labels as your identity, you stop observing the truth of what's really happening. You stop looking for the root causes—the stress, the fear, the unmet needs, the unspoken emotions—and instead accept the label as the end of the conversation. When you believe that anxiety or depression is something you "have," you become passive. You wait for it to go away, or worse, you assume it will always be a part of you. Instead of questioning to get to the root cause, you accept it as an unchangeable reality and turn to pills that dull the mind.

This is pulling you further away from seeing the reality of your situation. Medication becomes a quick fix, a way to numb the symptoms without ever addressing the cause. And while the pills may provide temporary relief, they also cloud your ability to observe the truth of what's happening inside you. They take the edge off the discomfort, but in doing so, they also dull the mind's natural inclination to investigate, to question, to dig deeper. You become less connected to yourself, less aware of the emotional and mental signals your body is sending.

The more you rely on medication, the further you drift from the real work that needs to be done and that's understanding the process of your thoughts and emotions. Instead of actively confronting the issues that are causing your *anxiety* or *depression*, you end up masking them, creating a fog around your mind that makes it even harder to see the truth.

By taking pills to cover up the symptoms, you lose the opportunity to fully understand what's driving those feelings in the first place. The mind becomes conditioned to look for easy escapes instead of engaging with the discomfort that's necessary for growth. You end up living in a constant state of avoidance, never truly addressing the root of your problems—and as a result, the cycle continues. The truth of your situation remains buried beneath the surface, hidden behind the labels, the medication, and the stories you've built around your experience.

Don't assume you know someone because of your history with them; people are consistently growing and evolving daily.

Take the label *wife* or *husband*. These roles come with certain expectations, behaviors, and responsibilities. But are you seeing your partner for who they truly are, or are you seeing them through the label of *wife* or *husband*? The moment we define something, we limit it. We stop seeing it for what it truly is and instead live within the constraints of the definition. We assume we know them when, in reality, they are constantly growing, changing, and evolving—or dying inside, feeling unseen. But the label says, *This is what it's supposed to be,* and so we stop learning about the person in front of us. We stop being curious, we stop observing, and we start living mechanically through the label.

When you label someone as *best friend* or *sibling*, you attach a set of expectations to that relationship. You assume that because they hold a certain place in your life, you know who they are. The people in your life are facing their own challenges, changing their views, and experiencing their own growth—or maybe they're struggling, feeling misunderstood, and you're too caught up in the label to notice. You think you know them because of the role they play in your life, but in reality, you're seeing them through the lens of what you *expect* them to be. You stop engaging with the person in front of you, relying on the label to do the work of understanding for you.

This can happen in all forms of relationships. You expect them to be the person you assume you know and when they show a different side of themselves, you're confused or disappointed. But the truth is, people are constantly going through experiences that can change one's perspective about life at any moment. The label just simplifies them in your mind. Living through labels diminishes the depth of every relationship. You miss out on the complexity, the growth, the struggles, and the realness of the people around you because you've locked them into a category. It's easier to categorize them with labels than to stay present, observe, and continuously learn who they are. It's more convenient to see your friend as the same person they were ten years ago than to engage with who they've become. But this is the danger of labels: they create distance, they create assumptions, and they prevent real connection.

If you're not constantly observing the people in your life, you'll start to drift away from them without even realizing it. The label tricks you into thinking you know them, but the truth is, if you stop paying attention, you'll lose sight of the person they've become. You'll wake up one day and realize you don't actually know them at all. When you're not present, you end up communicating with a version of them that no longer exists. This lack of awareness creates a gap. This is where the disconnect begins. Conversations become surface-level, misunderstandings grow, and eventually, you find yourselves on different pages entirely.

Being truly connected means observing, listening, and staying curious. It means seeing your partner, your friends, your family for who they are right now, not who they were or who you think they should be. It means asking questions, observing behavior, and being aware that the people in your life are constantly, psychologically, growing or dying daily. When you approach relationships with this mindset, you start to go beyond the label and start building connections on a deeper level.

Question everything. Don't question to agree or disagree, question to see the truth in what is being said for yourself.

What happens when you start to question the labels you've lived by? When you stop accepting words at face value and begin to see beyond the definition? Your mind becomes more alert, observant, fresh, aware, and alive. You stop living mechanically, and instead, you start living intentionally. You break free from the autopilot mode that labels put you in and start engaging with life in a deeper, more meaningful way. You become curious again, a student of life, constantly questioning, constantly learning. You start seeing things as they are—not as you've been conditioned to see them.

. . .

ASK YOURSELF: *Am I offended by the definition, or by the sound of the word? Am I living within the limitations of a label, or am I seeing things for what they really are? Am I lazy with my relationships? Do I actually know the people I claim to love the most?* When you strip away the definitions, what's left? What do you actually see? This process forces you to confront the assumptions and conclusions you've built your life around. This is where real growth happens. The truth is always being presented to you, moment by moment, but the question is: *Are you paying attention?*

Are you willing to challenge everything you've accepted as truth, or are you content living within the confines of your labels? The more you run from these questions, the more lost and confused you'll become. But if you choose to stop running and start observing, the truth will start to reveal itself, and you'll see that the labels you've been living by were just illusions.

11

UNFAIR ADVANTAGE

LEVERAGE AND PREPARATION

"Make yourself more valuable. The more you bring to the table, the less afraid you are to walk away from it."

The world is constantly evolving, and if you want to thrive, you must continuously increase your value. It means becoming someone who adds more to every room you enter, every conversation you engage in, and every opportunity you take on. Those who thrive aren't the ones who hold onto the old ways of thinking—they are the ones who adapt, evolve, and stay ahead of the game. You need to know where society is headed, and you must be aware of emerging trends, technologies, and shifts that are shaping the future. What worked yesterday might not work tomorrow. What was relevant last year could be gone by next year. You need to become someone who values leverage and preparation.

At the moment, automation and artificial intelligence (AI) are replacing entire industries. Jobs that once seemed secure are being outsourced or eliminated by technology. But it's not just blue-collar jobs—even highly specialized fields like law, medicine, and finance are being disrupted by advances in AI and machine learning. Understanding new technology is more than just being aware of the latest gadgets. It's about recognizing how these advancements will shape industries, impact economies, and transform the job market. The skills and tools that are relevant today may be gone in just a few years. Staying informed about technological trends allows you to stay adaptable and competitive.

One of the biggest shifts happening right now is the rise of cryptocurrency, especially Bitcoin. Bitcoin isn't just digital money—it's a complete game-changer in how we think about power, value, and control. Unlike traditional money, which is governed by banks and governments, Bitcoin is decentralized. No one entity has control over it. It runs on a technology called blockchain, a public ledger that keeps transactions secure and transparent. What makes Bitcoin revolutionary is that it cuts out the middleman. It gives power back to the individual—back to you. You need to see where the world is headed. The old ways of thinking, working, and exchanging value are quickly being replaced by something new.

We live in a time where social issues like diversity, inclusion, and equality are at the forefront of every major conversation. They are shaping the way businesses operate and how society interacts. Political decisions—from local governments to global policies—impact everything, from the economy to personal freedoms to job opportunities. Look at what happened during the COVID-19 pandemic. The entire world was thrown into chaos, and every aspect of life was disrupted. The lockdowns changed the way we work, interact, and live. This just shows how powerful political decisions are in shaping every aspect of your life.

Laws regulating technology, industry, trade, healthcare, and education are all shaped by politics. From how much you pay for groceries, to the interest rate on your mortgage, to raising your rent every year, to the kind of job opportunities available to you. If you don't understand these forces or how they impact your daily life, you will always be at the mercy of external factors. You will never feel fully in control or prepared.

Only a confused mind wants to return to what is old.

The world is forever changing, and you must change with it. You need to stay sharp, stay curious, and stay engaged. You must be educated and well-rounded. You can't be truly valuable if you're ignorant to how the world works. Read about opposing beliefs, challenge your thinking, and expand your worldview. Dive into history to understand how things have worked in the past and how they connect to the present. Study different religions and understand the importance of religion itself. The goal is not just to have knowledge for the sake of it but to understand the forces that move the world and the people in it.

Understand the game of money. You must learn what money truly is and how it works. Learn how to invest wisely, build your credit, leverage debt, learn how to do taxes, and study inflation, interest rates, crypto currency, and how to create multiple streams of income. Financial freedom is key to living a life on your own terms.

Dive into philosophy to explore the deeper questions about life, morality, and meaning. Just like this book, philosophy teaches you to question not just what you think, but how you think. It helps you identify biases, evaluate evidence, and consider all sides of an issue before forming an opinion. When you study philosophy, you're not just learning about theories or ideas; you're developing a mindset that allows you to navigate life with greater clarity and awareness.

Learn marketing and understand its importance. Marketing isn't just about selling products—it's also about selling ideas, personas, and even drama. Attention is power and many will say or do anything to get it. Understanding marketing gives you the awareness to see through this. You start to recognize the strategies at play—whether it's a brand trying to create urgency with a sale, a public figure stirring up controversy for views, or someone on social media portraying a life of perfection to gain followers.

You begin to see how people use marketing techniques to fool others into believing in something that isn't real. With this awareness, you stop falling for the drama and distractions. You realize that much of what people say or do is designed to get a reaction. It's all about controlling the narrative, shaping perception, and staying relevant. By understanding marketing, not only will you be able to create more opportunities for yourself, but you gain the ability to see beyond the surface and recognize the motives behind the messages people promote. You become more discerning, less easily influenced, and better equipped to focus on what truly matters.

Study health. If you want to live a life filled with energy, focus, and longevity, you must learn how to properly fuel it. Understanding health and fitness is the foundation for living a high-quality, productive life. When you take care of your body, you feel good and you look good, which builds more confidence. Your body is the vehicle through which you experience life, and taking care of it means you can handle challenges, perform at your best, and prevent long-term health issues like heart disease, diabetes, and mental health struggles. In a world filled with distractions, staying fit keeps you grounded, and understanding what's good for your body empowers you to make choices that enhance both your present and future self. Health is wealth.

Go train a martial art like boxing or jiu-jitsu. This is one of the most valuable skills you can develop for both your body and mind. It's not just about fighting—it's about gaining confidence, discipline, wisdom, and mental toughness. When you know how to defend yourself, you walk with a different kind of presence. You feel empowered, aware, and in control, which affects how you approach all areas of life. Martial arts teach you to stay calm under pressure and think strategically in the face of a challenge. It's not just about protecting yourself—it's about mastering yourself. You learn perseverance and how to control your emotions in high-pressure situations. That kind of confidence and self-awareness is priceless, making martial arts one of the most powerful tools for personal growth.

Studying human nature is one of the most valuable things you can do to increase your understanding of the world—and yourself. When you take the time to truly understand why people act the way they do, why women are the way they are, why men do what they do, you gain insight into the core drivers of behavior: fear, desire, insecurity, ambition, safety, and survival. Human nature is at the root of every decision, every interaction, and every social structure. Human nature doesn't change—it's been the same since the beginning of time. The same insecurities, the same drives, the same desires for power, connection, and survival have been driving human behavior for thousands of years. By studying it, you gain a deeper understanding of history, relationships, politics, business, and society at large. You see how these forces play out on a larger scale, influencing everything from economic systems to social movements.

Complacency is the enemy of growth.

Many people struggle with the choice to not engage with the world or educate themselves beyond their immediate surroundings. It's easy to get overwhelmed by the sheer volume of information out there—so much so that it feels like the best option is to shut it all out, to say, "Let me just focus on me." I know this first hand because I used to think that way too. I thought if I just locked in on my own life, focused on my immediate world, I could avoid the confusion and chaos that comes with constantly trying to keep up with everything around me. But here's the truth: there's a whole world out there, and whether we like it or not, it impacts us in ways we can't always see.

In a world of competition, why you? The economy, technology, politics, social trends—they all play a role in shaping our daily lives. Choosing to ignore these changes doesn't protect us from them. Instead, it leaves us vulnerable. It leaves us behind. The world doesn't stop evolving just because we've chosen to stop paying attention. When we choose not to educate ourselves, we're essentially choosing to remain blind to how the world works. We let ourselves get left behind because we think it's safer or less stressful. But what happens when the very changes we ignore come knocking on our door—when new technologies replace old jobs, when the economy shifts and we're unprepared, or someone breaks into your home and attacks you?

Choosing to not be educated is a form of self-sabotage and if we don't understand how it works, we end up suffering the consequences of that ignorance. Now, while some people are overwhelmed by the thought of educating themselves, others get caught up in the world's problems as a form of entertainment, not growth. They focus on what's going wrong in society, politics, or the news, but they do it without any personal transformation. It's a distraction—an excuse to avoid dealing with their own problems.

Make sure you get your life in order. You need to have a solid understanding of yourself, your goals, and your purpose. Once you've built that foundation, then you can see the world for what it truly is. With that solid base, you're in a position to bring value to the world in a real, meaningful way. You'll be contributing, not just consuming, and you'll be able to engage with the challenges around you from a place of strength and purpose.

Educate yourself, stay aware of the world's changes, but never lose sight of fixing your own world first. It's about being well-rounded, skilled, and adaptable. It means being the kind of person who brings something to the table no matter the situation. When you commit to becoming more valuable, you create opportunities, gain more respect, help more people, and set yourself apart from the average person who settles for mediocrity.

The more valuable you become, the more control you have over your life, your future, and the impact you make on the world. This isn't about perfection—it's about progress and preparation. Every next level of your life will demand a different version of you. So never settle, continue to level up, keep learning, and always make yourself an asset in every aspect of life.

12

HONOR YOUR WORD
THE FOUNDATION OF TRUSTING YOURSELF

"There's no such thing as being a perfect human being or living a perfect life. Live how you want to live. All conflict with yourself ends when you realize that you are free to choose how you want to live but you are not free from the consequences of your choices."

In a world full of empty promises and half-hearted commitments, actually doing what you say you'll do is a standout quality. Most people talk, but very few deliver. They set goals, make commitments, and throw out promises, but when the time comes to act, they fall short. Look around, inconsistency is everywhere. People flake, they cancel, they make excuses, and they rationalize why they didn't keep their word.

When you're the person who always shows up, always follows through, and always does what you say you'll do, you instantly become more valuable. People trust your word because they've seen you back it up with action constantly over time. It's more than just keeping promises —it's about who you are at your core. Your word is a reflection of your character, your integrity, and your commitment to yourself and others. The way you respect your word shapes how people see you and, most importantly, how you see yourself.

How you do anything is how you do everything.

Every small action you take reveals something about your character, whether you realize it or not. People may not say it out loud, but they can feel it. They can feel when you're cutting corners, when you're not giving your best, and when your words don't match your actions. People instantly know your character by the way you react and respond to whatever happens to you. They observe how you handle pressure, how you treat those around you, and how you show up when no one's watching.

It's all being documented, consciously or subconsciously, and it shapes how others perceive you. If you say you'll do something and don't follow through, it sends a message. It tells people that you don't value your own word, and they, in turn, won't either. Your reputation is built on the consistency of your everyday actions. If you slack off in one area of your life, it seeps into other areas. If you lack integrity with yourself, you'll lack it with others. Every reaction, every response, every follow-through (or lack of it) paints a picture of who you are and what you stand for.

When you commit to a standard of excellence in all areas of your life, people feel it. They see it in the way you carry yourself, the way you approach challenges, and how consistent you are with honoring your word. There's no hiding from the energy you put out—people can sense the difference between someone who just talks about it and someone who IS about it.

If you say you're going to do something, and then do

the opposite, it's a clear indicator of your reliability. It's in the small moments and the little commitments that your true character is revealed. If you tell someone you'll meet them at 8 P.M., do everything in your power to show up on time. If you borrow money and say you'll pay it back by a certain date, make sure you do. If you say you're going to wake up at 4 A.M. to hit the gym, then wake up at 4 A.M. and hit the gym.

It's not just about doing what you say—it's about your intention behind it. Yes, life happens, and sometimes things get in the way, but when your word is something you hold in high regard, you'll go out of your way to make things happen. And if something does come up, you communicate it clearly. You don't let things slide, because breaking your word should feel like committing a sin against your own integrity. When you operate with that level of respect for yourself and your word, it becomes a core part of who you are. It's no longer negotiable; it's a way of life.

When you trust yourself, it doesn't matter what happens.

Every time you follow through on what you say, you're not just fulfilling a commitment, you're building a foundation of self-belief. You're training your mind to rely on your own abilities and instincts, reinforcing the idea that when you say something, it will get done. It's the quiet confidence that comes from knowing that you're capable of delivering, no matter the circumstance. The more you honor your word, the more you reinforce this belief, and over time, you start to operate from a place of certainty rather than doubt.

When you trust yourself, it doesn't matter what happens. You believe in your ability to handle whatever comes your way, even when things get tough, even when the path is unclear. You've shown yourself time and time again that you'll figure it out. This kind of self-trust becomes a driving force behind everything you do. You take on bigger challenges because you've proven to yourself that you can handle them. You set more ambitious goals because you've established that you won't let yourself down. This trust spills into every area of your life. You start to make decisions faster, with more clarity, because you're not doubting yourself at every turn. You become more decisive, more focused, and more resilient.

When self-doubt creeps in, it doesn't control you anymore. You've built the muscle of follow-through, and that muscle is strong enough to push you through moments of uncertainty. When you show up with that kind of energy, people notice. They feel it in your presence. You become someone whose words carry weight because people know that you stand behind what you say.

Your reputation becomes one of reliability and action, and that opens doors. Opportunities come your way, not only because you've made the right moves to put yourself in a position to succeed, but because people trust you. They know that when you commit to something, you'll see it through. This reputation builds lasting relationships— personally and professionally. People want to work with you, to be around you, to invest in you, because they know that your word is backed by action.

Trusting yourself is part of the foundation of growth. It's what allows you to dream big, to take risks, and to face obstacles head-on because you've built a track record with yourself. You know you can handle whatever comes your way. And when you operate from that place of certainty, you're unstoppable. That's the kind of trust that creates real change, attracts real respect, and shapes the future you want.

Momentum is built moment to moment.

Momentum is the result of stacking these consistent actions together, and it begins to shape the way you approach every aspect of your life. Once that momentum kicks in, everything starts to fall into place. The goals that once seemed difficult or far away suddenly become easier to achieve because you've developed the habits and mindset necessary to handle them. Your life gains a sense of flow. You're no longer swimming against the current, but moving with it, carried by the momentum you've built through honoring your commitments.

This momentum creates *effortless success.* It doesn't mean the work is easy—it means that your approach to life becomes so aligned with your goals that it feels natural. You've removed the resistance that comes from self-doubt and inconsistency. Because you trust yourself to follow through, you stop wasting energy on procrastination, hesitation, and uncertainty. You've trained your mind to stay focused, which means you can approach challenges with a sense of calmness and clarity. The energy you used to waste on self-doubt and overthinking is now channeled into forward movement. There's no more psychological conflict because you've proven that you can be trusted to deliver.

When you don't honor your word, you spark a downward spiral of negative momentum. Every time you break a promise—whether to yourself or to others—you're chipping away at the foundation of self-trust that's critical for progress. It's not just about the immediate consequences of not following through; the real damage lies in how you begin to see yourself. You weaken the relationship you have with yourself. You start questioning your ability to deliver, not only on the promise you broke, but on anything you set out to achieve. It becomes harder to make decisions, to set goals, or to even trust your judgment. Suddenly, even simple tasks feel daunting because your mind is now wired to expect failure. This hesitation doesn't stay contained to the specific promise you didn't keep—it spreads, infecting your confidence and bleeding into your ability to act decisively in other areas.

You start to second-guess your actions, and that hesitation breeds inaction. You become trapped in a cycle of uncertainty, always wondering if you can really pull through. As this cycle continues, it doesn't just kill your self-confidence—it lowers your standards. You start accepting less from yourself. You rationalize why it's okay to cut corners, to settle for mediocrity, or to procrastinate. That initial failure to follow through becomes the new baseline for what you expect from yourself. You adjust downward, convincing yourself that it's normal to fall short.

This cycle of inaction and lowered standards eventually leads to deeper procrastination. You're no longer driven by the goals you once had or the potential you once saw in yourself. Instead, you're just trying to get by, avoiding commitments and challenges because you've lost the belief that you can handle them. Each time you don't follow through, you're reinforcing this negative cycle, making it harder to break free.

The longer this goes on, the more this mindset takes root. It creates a mental block that makes even the idea of starting something new feel overwhelming. You become stuck in a pattern of avoiding discomfort, afraid of further disappointment, so you don't even try. You're not just stuck in the same place—you're actively moving backward, away from the goals and progress you once set out to achieve.

To be clear, this isn't just about one missed deadline or one broken promise—it's about the mindset you're allowing to take over, one that reinforces inaction and lowered expectations. Breaking free from negative momentum is difficult because it requires a shift in your entire approach to life. You have to confront the discomfort you've been avoiding.

You have to rebuild the trust you've lost in yourself. You have to commit, once again, to honoring your word, and understand that each time you follow through, you're reversing the negative cycle. The longer you let this negative momentum build, the more it feels like you're swimming upstream, fighting against the limitations you've placed on yourself. But the moment you choose to honor your word again, you begin to change the tide. You start to rebuild the foundation of self-trust that leads to positive momentum, confidence, and forward progress.

You have to understand that people who follow through are rare; *being someone whose word holds weight is an asset.* It sets you apart. It makes you trustworthy, dependable, and respected. Your word is the foundation of your integrity, your character, and your reputation. Don't be a loser. If you say it, do it. Not just for others, but for yourself. Every time you honor your word, you are building the life you deserve. You are creating a future where people trust you, where you trust yourself, and where anything you set your mind to feels achievable.

13

NO WORDS

YOU WEAR YOUR MENTALITY

"We can all see you."

The most impactful communication happens without a single word being spoken. As you grow, improve, and elevate yourself, your energy begins to speak for you. It's not about what you say, but how you carry yourself, how you move, how you exist in a space. Your aura becomes a silent testament to the work you've put in, and others can feel it. You don't need to explain your progress—people will sense it.

In early human societies, communication wasn't always verbal. Before we had language, we relied on body language, energy, and presence. A person's posture, their walk, the way they looked others in the eye, and their movements all signaled who they were. You could tell who was confident, who was strong, who was fearful—without a single word. The way someone carried themselves signaled their status, intentions, and emotional state. A confident, upright posture could indicate leadership or readiness for battle, while slouched shoulders or avoiding eye contact might suggest submission or fear.

This form of communication was vital when humans lived in close-knit tribes, as it allowed for quick assessments of trust, strength, and reliability, especially in moments of danger or conflict. Presence was everything. You had to be attuned to the energy of those around you, sensing whether someone was an ally or an enemy, whether they were calm or agitated. You knew who was capable of protecting the group, who could be counted on, and who might crumble under pressure all without any verbal confirmation. In these times, your aura was your reputation, and your energy was your first form of communication. That primal ability to sense energy has never left us. Today, we still react to the unspoken. You've experienced it yourself: meeting someone who commands a room without speaking, or sensing when someone is hiding insecurity behind their words.

Don't be surprised when people treat you the same way you treat yourself.

As you elevate in life—physically, mentally, emotionally, financially—your growth becomes visible. People may not always be able to articulate what's different about you, but they'll feel it. You've changed, and it's undeniable. People will begin to say things like, "There's something different about you," or "You seem more confident." They'll respect you more, look to you for guidance, or even feel a sense of intimidation without understanding why. This is your growth radiating outward, making an impact without needing to be announced. The more committed you are to your growth, the less you need to prove yourself through words. Your energy, body language, and demeanor do the talking for you. There's a level of calm confidence that comes from knowing you've done the work—whether it's improving your skills, mastering your emotions, or leveling up in your career. You no longer feel the need to over-explain, justify, or seek validation because you've become the embodiment of your growth.

This energy shift will change the way others perceive you. Imagine walking into a room after leveling up your life. You're more grounded, more self-assured, and people notice. Your posture is straight, your movements deliberate, your eye contact is filled with certainty. People feel the difference, and the result is magnetic. Some will be drawn to you, wanting to know what changed, hoping to learn from your evolution. Others might be intimidated, unsure how to handle this new version of you. This shift in energy will naturally filter out those who don't align with your growth and attract those who do.

The beauty of allowing your energy to speak for you is that it increases your value exponentially. You no longer have to explain or sell yourself—your presence does that for you. You become a person of substance, someone who people respect and listen to, even before you've spoken a word. This is powerful because people trust what they can feel more than what they hear. Your authenticity, your integrity, your confidence—all of these become part of your silent communication, adding layers to your value without you having to say anything. In fact, speaking too much can kill and cheapen the energy a bit. When you are doing the work and leveling up, there's no need to broadcast it. Those who need to see it will, and those who don't are not meant to. Your growth will naturally create reactions—some people will be inspired, while others may feel uncomfortable with your progress because it forces them to confront their own stagnation.

But remember, none of this is about proving anything to anyone. Your focus should always be on being the best you can be in all areas of life. The world will react however it chooses. As you continue to grow, the impact you make without words will only strengthen. You'll find that opportunities start to come your way more frequently. People will want to be around you and collaborate with you because they can sense that you're someone who operates with integrity, confidence, and purpose.

No words, all moves.

14

QUALITY RELATIONSHIPS
RAISING YOUR STANDARDS

"When your priorities change so do your relationships."

Everything meaningful in life comes from the relationships we invest in. They shape who we are, influence the decisions we make, and form the foundation for how we move through life. Whether it's a romantic relationship, a friendship, or a business partnership, every connection you form plays a role in your journey. They are a mirror, reflecting your strengths, weaknesses, values, and insecurities. The quality of your relationships determines the quality of your life—how you feel about yourself, how you navigate challenges, and how you grow as a person. Every relationship has a purpose, whether you're conscious of it or not. People don't just come into your life randomly—there's always a reason, a foundation that forms the basis of the connection. Some relationships are rooted in growth, pushing you to become a better version of yourself. Others are based on comfort, providing a sense of stability but at the same time are keeping you stagnant. Then, there are relationships built on escapism—those that allow you to avoid confronting your own issues by surrounding yourself with distractions.

What is the foundation of the relationships in your life? What purpose do they serve, and how do they align with who you are and who you want to become? Are the relationships you've built an escape from dealing with deeper personal issues? Most people create connections based on their need to distract themselves from their own unresolved problems. These relationships might provide temporary relief from loneliness or insecurity, but they are not fulfilling.

They are surface level and most of the time end in disaster because they lack depth and authenticity. These are people who come together to avoid seeing themselves. In these types of relationships, there's little space for honesty, self-reflection, or personal growth. Addressing those uncomfortable truths would shatter the illusion, so instead, you both settle for a surface-level connection that avoids reality. It's a relationship of convenience, not one of true value. Instead of being a force for positive change, it becomes a distraction that keeps both parties stagnant.

Some relationships stem from a deep need for attention. If you aren't solid with yourself, you may find yourself craving validation from others to fill emotional voids. These connections are transactional—based on what you can get in terms of praise, acknowledgment, or approval. Once the flow of attention stops, the connection weakens because there was never real substance to begin with. These relationships are unstable because they rely on others to build up your self-worth, rather than you building it from within. When the constant validation fades, the relationship falls apart. You end up constantly seeking someone or something to fill a gap that can only be addressed by you.

Look at your relationships. Are you using relationships to avoid dealing with your own issues? Are you looking for others to fill an emotional void that you should be addressing yourself? When you chase validation through others, you're not forming genuine connections—you're creating temporary bonds that are easily broken the moment the attention fades. This leads to constant instability in your relationships and prevents real growth, both within yourself and with those around you. True lasting connections are built from a place of psychological strength, where you don't rely on others to define your worth, but instead, you add value to each other's lives through respect, and purpose.

**Look at most of the people around you.
Are these the most qualified people to be in your life?
Would you be around them if you were thriving on all levels?
A lonely mind settles for whatever is available, easy, and
cheap. The desperation has you giving your time, energy,
and attention to people you would instantly cut off the
moment you got your life together. Always move with a
vision, raise your level of self respect, and stop using people
while you figure out what you really want.**

It's important to understand the differences between meaningless and meaningful connections. Meaningless relationships are filled with inauthentic, low-quality people —those who use each other as a way to avoid looking inward. These connections might offer moments of fun or distraction, but they lack depth and substance. The laughter fades, the excitement dies down, and you're left feeling empty because these relationships were never built on anything real. Investing in people you can't build with will drain you. They provide distraction but offer no real value, keeping you trapped in cycles of avoidance and surface-level interactions.

Meaningful relationships are those that have depth. These are the connections that inspire you to be more, to grow, and to step into your full potential. When you're in a meaningful relationship, it's not just about how you feel in the moment; it's about how that relationship impacts your overall growth and journey. A quality friendship will support you and challenge you to see things from a new perspective pushing you to develop a deeper under-standing of the world. A romantic relationship backed by vision and purpose will inspire you to pursue personal goals with more determination because you know your partner supports your growth.

These relationships offer true value because they're based on the principle of mutual betterment. Being inten-tional about your relationships means evaluating them regularly. Are they still serving you? Are they helping you grow? Are they adding value to your life, or are they draining your energy? Relationships should elevate you, not pull you down. If you're surrounding yourself with people who are not aligned with your values or vision, it's time to reassess why they are still in your life.

You can't build anything meaningful with people who still struggle to find their own worth. If they don't value themselves, they'll sabotage every brick you lay.

Quality relationships push you to be better, challenge your mindset, and inspire you to evolve. They are grounded in truth, trust, passion, and love, offering a level of depth that fleeting or shallow connections simply can't provide. When two people or more come together with a shared mission, whether in friendship, romance, or business, the relationship becomes about more than just satisfying temporary desires. It serves a higher purpose—one that's focused on growth, development, and creating lasting value. These connections stick together through the ups and downs of life because they are not based on convenience or short-term gains but on a solid foundation of growth and support.

True, meaningful relationships are not driven by selfish needs or avoidance of personal issues—they are built on a foundation that uplifts everyone involved, allowing them to support each other's evolution and success. In these relationships, you're not just filling a gap—you're contributing to something bigger than yourself, and in doing so, you're constantly adding value to both your life and the lives of those around you. When you build relationships based on truth, purpose, and value, you create a network of high quality people. These relationships are not about filling emotional voids or escaping from reality—they are about building something greater together.

Solid relationships begin with oneself. You won't know what to do with a solid partner, team, or circle, if the foundation of the relationship you have with yourself is not solidified. Being the best version of you is what's best for everyone around you. Never stop working on you.

Most people are in desperate search for meaningful connections. The number one question I get asked over anything else you read in this book is: "How do I find quality, meaningful relationships?" The answer always starts with one simple truth: *quality relationships begin with you.* You don't attract what you want—you attract who you are.

Most people make the mistake of entering into relationships from a place of emotional lack, seeking validation, attention, or approval to fill a void. When you're unsure of who you are, or what you stand for, you will naturally attract people who may temporarily fill that void. But again, these people offer no real substance. If you're not solid with yourself, how can you expect to build something strong with someone else?

The foundation of every meaningful relationship starts with the relationship you have with yourself. When you are grounded in your own value, you approach relationships from a place of strength, not need. If you're not clear on your own identity, you'll settle for anyone and anything that comes your way. You'll attract people who reflect your own uncertainty, who seek comfort in the same things you're trying to escape from. But when you're truly grounded, when you understand who you are and what you bring to the table, everything shifts. You'll attract people who respect that value, and you'll recognize those who don't. You won't waste time on relationships that are temporary or on people who try to take more than they give. Instead, you'll be drawn to those who align with your purpose, your vision, and your mission.

Many people desire loyalty in their relationships, whether romantic, business, or friendships. What they fail to realize is that loyalty and honor are built on a foundation of integrity and self-respect, qualities that a struggling mind can't consistently provide. You must understand this: *A struggling mind can never be honorable.* Why? Because they're not operating from a place of clarity or strength. They're consumed with their own emotional conflicts, insecurities, and unresolved issues, making it impossible to offer the kind of loyalty that comes from genuine commitment and trust.

People often try to cut corners in this process. You expect loyalty from others without becoming someone worthy of that loyalty. You demand honesty, trust, and consistency from those around you, yet you haven't cultivated those qualities within yourself. When you haven't faced your own demons or resolved your struggles, you'll fall short when it matters most. You break promises, act out of fear, and betray others—even unintentionally—because your actions are driven by your unresolved pain, not by honor or loyalty.

Someone who doesn't trust themselves can't offer trust to others. They might say they're committed to a relationship but fail to show up when things get difficult, leaving the other person feeling abandoned or betrayed. Or they may seek loyalty from others but aren't able to offer it back because they're too focused on their own needs, seeking validation, or avoiding discomfort. A struggling mind is unreliable. It reacts impulsively, makes decisions based on short-term emotions, and seeks to avoid pain rather than face it. This creates a cycle of disappointment and betrayal —not because the person doesn't want to be loyal, but because they haven't built the foundation necessary to uphold loyalty in their actions. If you want loyalty in your relationships, you have to be loyal to yourself first. That means committing to your own growth, facing your inner struggles, and becoming someone who moves with integrity in everything you do. When you work on yourself —your mindset, your values, your emotional strength— you create a foundation that allows for deep, meaningful connections.

Look in the mirror, are you solid with who you are? Are you entering relationships from a place of strength, or are you looking for others to fill a void? If you want quality relationships in your life, you must first become the kind of person who attracts and sustains those relationships. The most valuable relationships serve a purpose beyond temporary fulfillment. They push you to grow, challenge your mindset, and inspire you to become more. When you are solid with yourself, the relationships you form will reflect that strength, leading to lasting, fulfilling connections that are built to withstand the ups and downs of life.

The fear of being lonely doesn't exist when you know the value you bring to the table.

Aim to be the most valuable person in the lives of those around you. This doesn't mean being manipulative or self-serving—it's about genuinely giving with the intention of helping, without expecting something in return. It's about consistently exceeding expectations and striving to add value in every interaction. People naturally gravitate toward those who bring real value, and the more you offer —whether it's support, advice, or simply your presence— the stronger your relationships will become.

You must understand your role in each relationship. Whether you're the friend, the business partner, the spouse, or even the mentor, ask yourself: *Am I being the best version of this role?* This is more than just showing up—it's about embodying the qualities that each relationship requires. Are you the one others can rely on for honesty, support, solutions, or guidance? Do you bring resources—whether they're emotional, intellectual, or practical—to the table? Being useful, reliable, and resourceful strengthens relationships because people know they can count on you in moments of need, but it also elevates your standing and reputation.

Value is built through consistency. Consistently being someone people can depend on, whether it's for advice, encouragement, or solving a problem, shows that you take your relationships seriously. It's about being the person who adds something meaningful in every interaction. When people know they can turn to you, not just for comfort but for clarity, action, and results, they'll naturally trust you more, lean on you more, and respect you at a deeper level. This is the foundation upon which strong, lasting relationships are built.

But it's not just about what you give—it's about *how* you give. The intention behind your actions matters. Are you giving to truly help, or are you giving with an expectation of something in return? Genuine giving—whether it's your time, energy, or resources—creates a deeper connection because people can sense authenticity. When your motivation is pure, the impact is far greater. It's not about grand gestures or trying to outshine others, but about offering value in ways that are thoughtful and meaningful.

The quality of your giving is just as important as the act itself. When you give from a place of abundance and care, the energy you put out is felt by everyone around you. Are you present in the moment when you offer support, or are you distracted, half-engaged? Are you giving because it's expected, or because you genuinely want to contribute? The difference is noticeable, and it shapes the way people perceive and respond to you. Giving in the right way means understanding the needs of the other person. It's not about pushing your help on someone, but about listening, being attentive, and offering what's truly valuable to them. Sometimes, the best way to give is through a kind word, a listening ear, a hug or just being there when they need you. It's about being aware of the other person's needs and responding in a way that supports their growth and well-being.

How you give defines your character and builds trust.

When people know that your contributions come from a genuine place, they'll respect you more, trust you more, and feel more connected to you. This is what makes relationships thrive—consistent, authentic, and thoughtful giving that enhances the lives of those around you. However, it's important to not overdo it. When you overdo it and try to be there for others for all the wrong reasons—whether it's out of insecurity, a need to be liked, to look cool or to fit in—you can come across as desperate for approval.

This lowers your value because it shows you're giving from a place of emotional lack rather than strength. When people sense you're seeking affirmation through over-giving, they may start to take advantage of your generosity, opening the door for manipulation and being taken advantage of. Instead of being seen as valuable, you are being viewed as someone who can be easily used. True value comes from giving with intention, not from overextending yourself to meet others' expectations or to fill a void within yourself.

Being valuable means you're selective about where you invest your energy. Prioritize depth over what is cheap and temporary. Make sure your actions and contributions are meaningful and genuine, and the people who matter will recognize your value. By consistently being valuable and dependable, you elevate not only your relationships but also your reputation and sense of self-worth. You'll start to see yourself as someone who brings real value to the table. This is how you create a network of solid, authentic relationships that can stand the test of time—connections that are based on growth, trust, and long-term value.

Masculine vs. Feminine Energy: Relationship Dynamics

Understanding the foundation of masculine and feminine energy is essential for creating healthy, meaningful relationships. These energies exist in all of us, regardless of gender, and they shape how we relate to one another. Masculine energy is typically associated with traits like assertiveness, focus, and a drive for action. It's the energy of doing, of pushing forward, of taking charge. Feminine energy, on the other hand, embodies qualities like nurturing, intuition, and receptivity. It's the energy of being, of listening, of flowing with the situation. The phrase "opposites attract" is rooted in the natural balance between these energies.

In a harmonious relationship, masculine and feminine energies complement each other, creating a dynamic that allows each person to thrive in their role. For instance, a masculine individual may bring direction and structure, while a feminine person brings creativity and emotional insight. Together, they form a partnership where both strengths are honored and balanced. In romantic relationships, this balance is especially important. A masculine man is drawn to the soft, nurturing energy of a feminine woman, and vice versa. The feminine energy softens, supports, and inspires the masculine to achieve its highest potential, while the masculine energy provides security, focus, and leadership to the feminine. This balance creates harmony because both partners are playing roles that naturally align with their energy.

There is instant conflict when two people in a relationship embody the same dominant energy. For example, when two highly masculine individuals come together, there can be a constant struggle for power and control. Both people want to lead, make decisions, and take charge, leading to friction and conflict. Conversely, if two people are both highly feminine, the relationship may lack direction and action. Neither person is taking the initiative, leading to stagnation and frustration.

This isn't about gender or stereotypes—it's about understanding the energies that govern your interactions. In any relationship, whether it's romantic, professional, or social, there is always a dominant energy at play. Recognizing your own natural energy helps you align with people who balance and complement you. If you're naturally more masculine, you'll thrive with someone who brings more feminine energy and vice versa. This doesn't mean you have to suppress who you are or try to be someone you're not—it simply means being aware of the dynamics in your relationships. The more you grow and become aware of your natural energy, the more you'll start to notice the underlying patterns in your relationships.

When you are true to yourself, aligning with the energy that is authentic, relationships flow with much more ease and direction. This is because you're not forcing a role or dynamic that doesn't come naturally to you. Trust me, I know how all this *energy* talk can sound—I'm not trying to get all spiritual or throw around abstract ideas. But here's the truth: this concept of masculine and feminine energy, and how it plays out in relationships, is rooted in the dynamics we see every day. Whether you believe in it or not, energy balance is always at play. It's not about being mystical or 'airy fairy'—it's about understanding how natural forces shape our behavior, desires, and compatibility. When two dominant energies come together, there's tension. When one person is passive and the other is assertive, there's a natural flow. These dynamics aren't some abstract, spiritual concept—they're basic observations about human behavior.

For example, a dominant woman may fantasize about being with a masculine man, but in reality, the masculine man won't see her as compatible. Why? Because both are trying to occupy the same space—the space of control, leadership, and direction. That constant push and pull creates conflict. It's not about anyone being right or wrong; it's about understanding that certain energies complement each other better than others. This isn't about putting people in boxes. If you're naturally assertive, you will clash with someone who's equally assertive. If you're nurturing and intuitive, you'll align better with someone who complements that with focus and direction.

When you embrace your natural energy, you start to attract relationships that flow instead of fight. This is why it's so important to understand the role energy plays in relationships. Once you get that, things start to make more sense. You stop wondering why certain relationships feel like a constant battle. You see the patterns for what they are—imbalances in energy. It's not about one person being better than the other, but about finding the dynamic that works. The more you align with your authentic self, the more fulfilling your relationships will be.

A highly feminine woman may feel drained or unsupported if she's in a relationship with a man who embodies a lot of feminine energy. She may crave the structure, focus, and leadership that a masculine energy brings, but if her partner isn't providing that, she may feel lost or directionless. You must recognize that energy balance is not something you can escape. Whether you like it or not, it's always at work. No matter how much you fantasize about a different dynamic, the laws of energy remain constant. If you're constantly battling for control in your relationships, or if you're feeling unfulfilled, it's likely because the balance of energies is off. It's crucial to align with your authentic energy and to seek partners and relationships that complement it, not clash with it.

Be careful with those who are flexible with their identity. Nothing is solid with these people. They will become what the room needs them to be and switch up on you the moment it's time to fill another void. Trust those who have strong, positive (non-negotiable) core values. These people will accept the consequences that comes with being who they are.

It's important to note that no one is purely masculine or feminine. We all have a blend of both energies, and different situations call for different expressions. Understanding when to access each energy allows you to navigate life more effectively and form more harmonious relationships. In every relationship, whether it's a romantic partnership, a friendship, or a business connection, you are either more dominant or more submissive. One person leads; the other follows. One person pushes forward, while the other supports. This ebb and flow of energy creates a balance that allows the relationship to thrive.

However, when someone stops playing their role, there will be conflict within the relationship. For instance, in a relationship where the man is the natural leader, if he suddenly becomes passive and unsure of himself, the woman may be forced to take on the masculine role. This shift can cause confusion and resentment because it disrupts the natural energy balance. The attraction may begin to fade because the roles that once brought balance are no longer being fulfilled. When you ignore your natural energy, you attract people who are incompatible with your true self. Whether you are more masculine or feminine, there's serious power in fully embodying your role. When you embrace who you are, you naturally attract the right people into your life—those who complement your energy and help you grow. You also become more valuable in every relationship because you bring something unique and important to the table.

It's important to recognize that this doesn't mean you must remain fixed in one role. Masculine and feminine energy are fluid, and you may need to shift between them depending on the situation. However, knowing your dominant energy allows you to navigate relationships with greater clarity and purpose. At the core of every successful relationship is an understanding of the dynamic between masculine and feminine energy. These energies, when aligned, create a powerful synergy that elevates both individuals. Relationships flourish when each person fully embraces their role, and balance is maintained. By understanding your own energy and recognizing it in others, you gain clarity and insight into how to approach every relationship in your life. The better you understand these dynamics, the more valuable you become—not just in romantic relationships, but in friendships, business partnerships, and every other connection you form. When you become more of what you are, everything falls into place.

15

ALIVE

THE END IS THE BEGINNING

"This game is never ending. As long as you are alive you will be challenged. You will fail. You will have setbacks and no matter how much you think you know, you will never know it all. You must continue to grow, study, question, and make adjustments."

Y ou are reading this book for a reason. Up until this point, you've been in the *negative*. It means you've been operating from a place of deficiency, lacking clarity, struggling with confusion, and overwhelmed by the unresolved problems in your life. When you're in the negative, the goal is to get to *Zero*, to break even, to feel like you're back in control. Being in the negative might mean you've been distracted, lost, unclear, overwhelmed or frustrated. Maybe you've struggled with financial difficulties, relationships, bad habits, or a lack of purpose. You might have felt stuck in repetitive cycles, battling with the feeling that life is passing you by. You may have experienced loneliness, depression, or anxiety, all the while wondering why you couldn't break free from your own psychological limitations. Maybe you've been chasing validation, seeking approval from others, or endlessly comparing yourself to people around you, always feeling like you're behind. Your confidence may have been shattered by past failures, rejections, or setbacks, leaving you questioning your worth, your abilities, and your place in this world. Maybe you feel like life is over or you're too old or it's too late. You've numbed the pain with distractions—social media, alcohol, drugs, video games, meaningless relationships—always looking for a way to escape the discomfort you felt inside.

This is what it means to be in the *negative*. It's living from a place of lack, where nothing feels enough because you haven't addressed the deeper problems. You've been building your life on top of avoidance, hoping that if you just work hard enough or distract yourself long enough, the problems will disappear. But they won't. You can't build a solid foundation for thriving relationships, successful businesses, or a meaningful life if your mind is still full of unresolved issues. You can't ignore these problems and try to move forward as if they don't exist. This isn't about feeling discouraged or having a victim mindset. It's about recognizing that before you can truly thrive, you need to confront the things that have been holding you down.

Whatever brought you here—whether it was frustration, failure, heartbreak, or a burning desire for more—it all had to happen in order for you to be here with me right now. All of it served a purpose. Now what are you going to do? Right here, right now, you're at a place where you can rebuild from the ground up, with new knowledge, perspective, and intention. You've learned how to break free from the distractions, the illusions, and the limiting beliefs that once kept you in the negative. Now, you stand on a solid foundation, armed with clarity and purpose.

Every lesson, every principle you've absorbed, has prepared you for this moment. You are no longer looking to escape. You are no longer reacting to life; you are creating it. You've opened your mind to a new way of thinking, a way that prioritizes truth, purpose, and intentional living. Now, it's time to rebuild. It's time to redefine who you are and what your life is going to be. You now see the world for what it truly is. You understand that most people are lost in their own illusions, trapped in confusion, and driven by emotions they don't even understand.

But you're not like them anymore. *You're above the illusion now.* You've risen above the noise. You've stripped away the layers of confusion and distraction that once held you back. You are sharp. You're clear. You move with purpose. You are not easily discouraged. You move without fear because you know there's a higher power protecting and watching over you. You don't get caught up in unnecessary conflicts, emotional outbursts, or distractions that don't serve you. You are calm. You keep patience at the forefront of your mind because you know that every moment is an opportunity to move with precision and clarity.

You're a leader now. You understand that everything you do sets an example, whether you're aware of it or not. You don't just take care of yourself; you take care of your family, your friends, your circle. You're building a new legacy. You're breaking cycles of limitation, lack, and confusion. You're creating a future that's based on purpose, integrity, and responsibility. Everything you do matters. Every choice, every action, every conversation, every thought to the way you treat yourself and others. The content you consume, the music you listen to, the TV shows you watch, the podcasts that fill your mind—everything plays a role in shaping who you are becoming. This is no longer just about entertainment or distraction. You've changed the meaning of fun.

Fun is no longer about temporary distractions, mindless indulgence, or cheap thrills. It's no longer about wasting time just to escape the discomfort of facing your own reality. Fun now means growth. Fun now means doing things that elevate you, that challenge you, that sharpen your skills and expand your mind. Fun is becoming better every day. It's finding joy in the process of learning, of pushing your limits, of discovering what you're truly capable of and in gratitude. You've redefined fun as something that adds to your life, not something that drains it.

Preparation is now a priority. In all areas of life—financially, mentally, physically—you're always preparing, always positioning yourself to thrive. You are a forward thinker, always three steps ahead. You're no longer afraid of failure because you understand that failure is the greatest teacher of them all. Every setback is a lesson, every mistake is a step toward mastery. You embrace challenges, knowing that they are refining you, sharpening you, and bringing you closer to your goals. You lead by example. You no longer feel the need to prove yourself to anyone. You don't seek validation or approval from others because your actions speak for themselves.

People watch you, they feel your presence, and they are inspired by the way you live your life. You've become someone others look to for guidance—not because you demand it, but because you've earned it. You live with intention, and your energy naturally draws others to you. You are now responsible for planting seeds of understanding on to others. You don't tell people what to see. Instead, you point them in the right direction and allow them to discover the truth for themselves. Your life is the message. You show people what's possible by living a life of integrity, discipline, and purpose. You lift others up, not by telling them what to do, but by showing them the way through your own actions. You bring people up with you, not by dragging them, but by walking your own path so powerfully that they are inspired to follow. You honor your word. Your word holds weight because when you say you're going to do something, you do it.

Your relationships are intentional. You've outgrown the meaningless, surface level relationships that once drained your energy and replaced them with connections that inspire, challenge, and elevate you. Every relationship you have now is a reflection of the work you've done on yourself. Your connections are filled with the kind of value that only comes from living with clarity and direction. The way you communicate is clear, direct, and meaningful. The way you move through the world is calm, confident, and composed. You are well-prepared in all areas of life.

You don't run from your problems anymore. You face them head-on, knowing that avoiding them only delays your growth. You understand that you have to be solid with yourself before you can be solid with anyone else. This means you handle your business, take care of your responsibilities, and ensure that everything you do aligns with your highest values. You are someone people can count on. You show love to those who have been with you from the start, and you bring them with you as you grow. You never forget the people who supported you along the way, and as you rise, you make sure they rise with you.

You are changing the family tree, setting a new standard for what's possible. From this point on, you are responsible for your impact. Your life is no longer just about you. It's about the example you set, the seeds you plant, and the people you uplift. You lead, not by trying to control others, but by controlling yourself—your thoughts, your emotions, and your actions. You are now a living blueprint of what's possible when you move with intention. This is your foundation. You've stripped away the distractions, the confusion, the illusions, the negative cycles that held you back. Now, what will you create? What legacy will you leave behind? How will you live, knowing that every moment matters? You are the example. You are alive. The world is watching.

FROM HERE, now you build.

ABOUT THE AUTHOR

Anthony Minaya is a philosopher, martial artist, entrepreneur, and life coach. Born and raised in The Bronx, New York, Anthony grew up in a Puerto Rican and Dominican household, surrounded by environments where mediocrity was the norm and just getting by was the goal. Anthony wasn't fighting rock bottom he was battling comfort zones, low standards, victim philosophy, and the mediocrity that traps most people. This reality led him to ask one question: "Does life really have to be this way?" His desire to break free pushed him to dive deep into human psychology, personal growth, and self mastery. For almost two decades Anthony has personally worked one-on-one with hundreds of individuals and influenced thousands online by dissecting human nature, exposing the illusions that hold people hostage, and teaching others how to break free from the perspectives that keep them small. Anthony's mission is to shift how you see yourself and the world—reconstructing the way you think, so you walk with certainty, own every space you enter, and stand behind every decision you make.

www.anthonyminaya.com

instagram.com/anthonyminaya1

Made in the USA
Columbia, SC
04 May 2025

57524747R00079